Woman's Dress

A Collection of Vintage Articles on Dressmaking, Millinery and Tailoring

By

Various Authors

British Library Cataloguing-in-Publication Data
A catalogue record for this book is available from
the British Library

Dressmaking and Tailoring

Dressmaking and Tailoring broadly refers to those who make, repair or alter clothing for a profession. A dressmaker will traditionally make custom clothing for women, ranging from dresses and blouses to full evening gowns (also historically called a mantua-maker or a modiste). Whereas a tailor will do the same, but usually for men's clothing - especially suits. The terms essentially refer to a specific set of hand and machine sewing skills, as well as pressing techniques that are unique to the construction of traditional clothing. This is separate to 'made to measure', which uses a set of pre-existing patterns. Usually, a bespoke tailored suit or dress will be completely original and unique to the customer, and hence such items have been highly desirable since the trade first appeared in the thirteenth century. The Oxford English Dictionary states that the word 'tailor' first came into usage around the 1290s, and undoubtedly by this point, tailoring guilds, as well as those of cloth merchants and weavers were well established across Europe.

As the tailoring profession has evolved, so too have the methods of tailoring. There are a number of distinctive business models which modern tailors may practice, such as 'local tailoring' where the tailor is met locally, and the garment is produced locally too, 'distance tailoring', where a garment is ordered from an out-of-town tailor, enabling cheaper labour to be used - which, in practice can now be done on a global scale via e-commerce websites, and a 'travelling tailor', where the man or woman will travel between cities, usually stationing in a luxury hotel to provide the client the same tailoring services they would provide in their local store. These processes are the same for both women's and men's garment making.

Pattern making is a very important part of this profession; the construction of a paper or cardboard template from which the parts of a garment are traced onto fabric before cutting our and assembling. A custom dressmaker (or tailor) frequently employs one of three pattern creation methods; a 'flat-pattern method' which begins with the creation of a sloper or block (a basic pattern for a garment, made to the wearer's measurements), which can then be used to create patterns for many styles of garments, with varying necklines, sleeves, dart placements and so on. Although it is also used for womenswear, the 'drafting method' is more commonly employed in menswear and involves drafting a pattern directly onto pattern paper using a variety of straightedges and curves. Since menswear rarely involves draping, pattern-making is the primary preparation for creating a cut-and-sew woven garment. The third method, the 'pattern draping method' is used when the patternmaker's skill is not matched with the difficulty of the design. It involves creating a muslin mock-up pattern, by pinning fabric directly on a dress form, then transferring the muslin outline and markings onto a paper pattern or using the muslin as the pattern itself.

Dressmaking and tailoring has become a very well respected profession; dressmakers such as Pierre Balmain, Christian Dior, Cristóbal Balenciaga and Coco Chanel have gone on to achieve international acclaim and fashion notoriety. Balmain, known for sophistication and elegance, once said that 'dressmaking is the architecture of movement.' Whilst tailors, due to the nature of their profession - catering to men's fashions, have not garnered such levels of individual fame, areas such as 'Savile Row' in the United Kingdom are today seen as the heart of the trade.

Millinery

Whereas 'hatmaking' is the manufacture of hats and headwear, 'millinery' also encompasses the *designing* and manufacture of hats. A milliner's store, predictably, is a shop which sells those goods. Historically, milliners, typically female shopkeepers, produced or imported an inventory of garments for men, women, and children, including hats, shirts, cloaks, shifts, caps, neckerchiefs, and undergarments, and sold these garments in their millinery shop. More recently, the term has evolved to refer specifically to someone who designs and makes hats, usually primarily for a female clientele. The origin of the term is likely the Middle English *milener*, an inhabitant of Milan or one who deals in items from this Italian city, known for its fashion and clothing.

Many styles of headgear have been popular through history and worn for different functions and events. They can be part of uniforms or worn to indicate social status. Styles include the top hat, hats worn as part of military uniforms, cowboy hat, and cocktail hat. Perhaps the most recent popular incarnation is the fascinator; a style which uses feathers, stylish materials, beads, pearls and crystals - ranging from extravagant to petite for brides, weddings, christenings, ladies' day at the horse races and many other glamorous occasions.

Notable Milliners include the German born Anna Ben-Yusuf (1845-1909), who wrote *The Art of Millinery* (1909), one of the first reference books on millinery technique. It was formatted as a series of lessons, each dealing with a particular aspect of constructing a hat, treating the fabric or creating different types of trimming. Ben-Yusuf also set up her own school of millinery, based in Boston and New York. On a more practical note, it also advised on correct storage, renovating fabrics, and the business side of millinery, and included a glossary of terms. Subsequently, milliners such as Lilly Daché have achieved notable success. This French designer made hats for many Hollywood films and movie stars, including Marlene Dietrich, Caroline Lombard and Loretta Young. Her major contributions to millinery were draped turbans, brimmed hats molded to the head, half hats, visored caps for war workers, coloured snoods, and romantic massed-flower shapes.

Today, designers such as Philip Treacy and Stephen Jones are at the forefront of the millinery profession. Jones especially is considered one of the world's most radical and important milliners, also one of the most prolific, having created hats for the catwalk shows of many leading couturiers and fashion designers, such as John Galliano at Dior and Vivienne Westwood. His work is known for its inventiveness and the high level of technical expertise with which he realises his ideas.

WOMAN'S DRESS

Conducted by the Editress of "Fashions for All"

In this important section of EVERY WOMAN'S ENCYCLOPÆDIA every aspect of dress will be dealt with by practical and experienced writers. The history of dress from earliest times will be told, and practical and useful information will be given in :

Home Dressmaking		Millinery
How to Cut Patterns	*Home Tailoring*	*Lessons in Hat Trimming*
Methods of Self-measure-	*Representative Fashions*	*How to Make a Shape*
ment	*Fancy Dress*	*How to Curl Feathers*
Colour Contrasts	*Alteration of Clothes, etc.*	*Flowers, Hat-pins, Colours, etc.*

Boots and Shoes	**Furs**	**Gloves**
Choice	*Choice*	*Choice*
How to Keep in Good Condition	*How to Preserve, etc.*	*Cleaning, etc.*
How to Soften Leather, etc.	*How to Detect Frauds*	**Jewellery, etc.**

PRACTICAL LESSONS IN DRESSMAKING
By M. PRINCE BROWNE

Examiner in Dressmaking, Tailoring, French Pattern Modelling, Plain Needlework, and Millinery, of the Teachers in Training at the University College of South Wales and Monmouthshire, Cardiff ; the London Higher Technical Examination Centres, etc. ; First Class Diploma for Tailoring ; Diploma of Honour for Dressmaking ; Diploma of Merit of the Highest Order for Teaching ; Silver Medallist, London Exhibition, 1900 ; Silver Medal, Franco-British Exhibition, 1908 ; Author of " Up-to-Date Dresscutting and Drafting," also " The Practical Work of Dressmaking and Tailoring."

PART I.—Appliances necessary for Dressmaking

A succession of these practical lessons in Dressmaking will appear in the following parts of EVERY WOMAN'S ENCYCLOPÆDIA. The first task before us is to consider the appliances necessary.

SEWING MACHINE

A "LOCK STITCH" machine is the best, as the work is stronger and more secure, and the stitching is not so clumsy as when done by a "chain stitch" machine.

SKIRT BOARD

A skirt board is a great help in tacking the material and lining of a skirt together, and it is almost a necessity for pressing the seams. These boards can be had from 4s. 6d. each.

SLEEVE BOARD (Single or Double)

A sleeve board for pressing the seams of sleeves, etc., can also be purchased from 1s. 6d. A small size must be selected, or it will not pass through the cuff of a blouse, or the bottom of a sleeve (see diagrams in the tailoring article). If expense has to be considered, a wooden rolling-pin, costing about 4½d., can be used instead of a sleeve board, or even a roller from a round towel will do as a substitute.

FLAT IRONS, IRON STAND

Two or three flat irons are necessary for pressing the seams, etc. They should weigh about three or four pounds. They can be obtained from any ironmonger, and cost from 8d. each.

For delicate work a "shoe," to slip over the iron after it is heated, to prevent its scorching or soiling the material, is desirable. It can be purchased for 1s. at any good ironmonger's.

IRONING BLANKET

Before pressing the garment which is being made, an ironing blanket should be placed over the board or table.

DRESS STAND

A padded dress stand is the best, and one covered with drill is the strongest. They can be had in stock sizes or made to measure from a well fitting bodice. An arm, or arms, for the dress stand is a great addition ; but this need not be purchased, it can be made by the worker at the cost of only a few pence as follows : A sleeve should be cut in stout holland and fitted *tightly* to the arm (the arm should be held in a slightly bent position). When fitted, the seams must be machine-stitched. A small oval shaped piece of holland must be cut out (allowing sufficient for turnings all round) to fit the bottom of the sleeve. It should be turned down and firmly sewn in all round to fill in the bottom of the sleeve. The sleeve should then be stuffed with sawdust, *very firmly* pressed in, to give the sleeve the shape of the arm.

When the sleeve is quite full, another oval piece of holland must be cut with turnings, turned down, and sewn in all round to fill in the *top* of the sleeve in the same way as the smaller piece at the wrist.

Both the *right* and *left* arm can be made in this way if desired, and will be found a great help in the draping of sleeves.

CUTTING-OUT SCISSORS, BUTTONHOLE SCISSORS, NEEDLES

The most useful sizes for needles are 5 to 9, and if a dress is to be boned, No. 4 " between " needles are the best.

PINS, STEEL PINS, AND TAPE MEASURE

Fine steel pins are the best for pinning velvet and silk, as they do not mark the material as ordinary pins do.

TRACING WHEEL (Dia. 1)

A single one is best, and is used for marking seams, etc. It costs 1s.

N.B.—A double wheel costs more and is not nearly so good, as they are made to mark both the lines of stitching and the width for the turning ; but as all seams do not require the same width of turning to be left on them, and the width of turning also varies with the material, it is better to use a *single* wheel and to leave the *necessary* turning.

PUSH PINS (Dia. 2)

These are most useful for fixing a paper pattern to the lining, etc., flat on the table, or board, ready to be outlined with the tracing wheel.

Tracing Wheel Dia. 1

The push pins have needle points, and do not leave a mark on the material. If ordinary pins are used

Push Pin Dia. 2

the pattern is frequently " puckered " on the lining or material, and cannot be outlined so accurately.

These push pins are sold in boxes of one dozen for 5d. a box.

PINKING IRON, MALLET, LEAD (Dia. 3)

Silk frills can be " pinked " out round the edge, if required, by the home worker herself if a pinking iron, wooden mallet, and a piece of lead are purchased.

The pinking irons cost from about 9d. each, according to the size of the scallop. The lead is sold by weight (a small piece is sufficient). The mallet should

Pinking Iron Dia. 3

be made of boxwood, or it will soon split; it costs about 2s. or 2s. 6d.

For further appliances, see next article on Tailoring.

PART II

Materials, etc., necessary for Dressmaking. Material for making the desired Garment. Suitable Lining (if a Lining is desired).

TACKING COTTON

This cotton can be bought in reels of 1,000 yards in various numbers. The price is from 2¾d. per reel, according to the number.

MACHINE AND SEWING COTTON, SEWING AND MACHINE SILK

If the garment is to be entirely stitched with silk, it is more economical to buy it in quarter-ounce reels, price 5d. each. Another advantage is that the silk on this size reel can be had in *various* thicknesses. If only a small quantity of silk is required, the ordinary 1½d. reels can be used. They are usually very fine, and are suitable for stitching thin materials and for hemming, oversewing, etc.

BUTTONHOLE TWIST

This can be bought either by the yard or in penny reels in any colour. That on the reels is all of one size, but the twist sold by the yard is of various thicknesses, and is from 1d. a yard, according to the thickness.

Buttonhole twist is used for the working of eyelets, loops, embroidering eyes, stitching on hooks and eyes, also for " fanning " bones, stitching in tight bands, cross-stitch for marking the centre of skirt bands, etc., as well as for working buttonholes.

Twist to *match* the dress should be used for working the buttonholes, eyelets, eyes, and loops. For stitching hooks and eyes on to *bands* it should be black or white, to match the band.

For " fanning " the bones, stitching in the tight band, and the cross-stitch for marking the centre of the skirt band, twist of a contrasting colour is generally used.

HOOKS AND EYES, ETC.

These are of various kinds. The ordinary hooks are sold in packets at 1d. each or two for 1½d., and in different sizes.

HUMP HOOKS AND LACE HOOKS

These are usually sold on cards. Any of the above can be used for bodices and blouses.

Mantle hooks are sold on cards at 2d. or 3d. per card, according to quality. These, besides being used for cloaks, wraps, etc., are useful for fastening bands of skirts, but they must be of a small size for this purpose, or they will be too bulky.

These small sized mantle hooks are only made in the best quality at 3d. per card.

PATENT FASTENERS

These are used for fastening placket-holes, also blouses, etc. They close more securely and invisibly than ordinary hooks and eyes, and are of various kinds.

The first practical lessons to be given in Part 2 of EVERY WOMAN'S ENCYCLOPÆDIA

2

PRACTICAL LESSONS IN TAILORING
FOR HOME WORKERS AND OTHERS
By M. PRINCE BROWNE

Examiner in Dressmaking, Tailoring, French Pattern Modelling, Millinery, and Plain Needlework of the Teachers in Training at the University Colleges of South Wales and Monmouthshire, Cardiff, the London Technical Examination Centre. etc. Author of " Up-to-Date Dresscutting and Drafting," also " The Practical Work of Dressmaking and Tailoring."

I. THE APPLIANCES NECESSARY FOR TAILORING

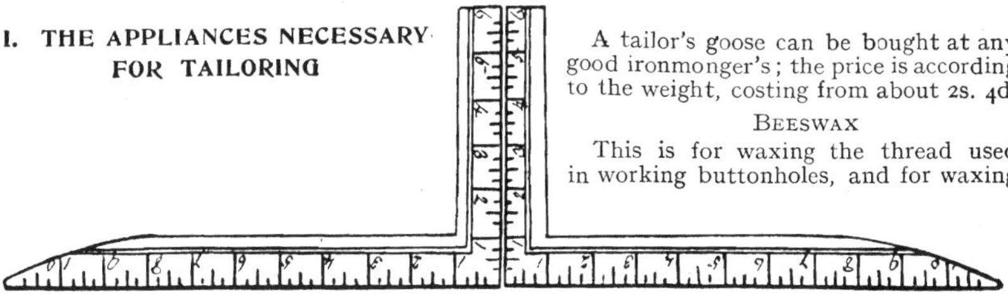

Diagrams 1 and 2
TAILOR'S SQUARES

Two Squares are necessary (placed in the position denoted in diagrams 1 and 2) for drafting the seams of skirts and of long coats. The price of the squares is 2s. each.

Diagram 3
TAILORS' CHALK (White and Coloured).

Tailors' chalk, used for marking out, can be obtained for about 3d. per dozen the best quality.

Diagram 4
TAILOR'S BODKIN

This is used for perfecting the round hole at the end of a buttonhole after it is worked.
It can be bought at any tailor's trimming shop for 1d.

Diagram 5
TAILOR'S GOOSE

Two of these irons are necessary, weighing from 8 pounds to 12 pounds each. These are essential for the successful pressing of tailor-made garments—flat-irons are not sufficiently heavy.

A tailor's goose can be bought at any good ironmonger's ; the price is according to the weight, costing from about 2s. 4d.

BEESWAX

This is for waxing the thread used in working buttonholes, and for waxing sewing silk to strengthen it. A piece of yellow wax, at 1d. or 2d., is sufficient, and can be had from any chemist or oilshop. The next appliances necessary are :

CUTTING-OUT SCISSORS
BUTTONHOLE SCISSORS

Diagram 6
A LEATHER PUNCH

This punch is used for cutting the round hole at the end of each buttonhole ; also for cutting eyelet-holes. There are various-sized " points '" for a punch ; No. 5 is the most useful. It can be obtained for 1s. 6d. complete. Extra " points " can be had for 3d. each.

A regular buttonhole punch is far more expensive, and not so useful as a leather punch and a pair of buttonhole scissors. We now require :

PINS—NEEDLES—THIMBLE

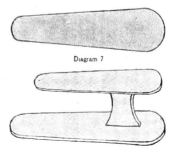

Diagram 7

Diagram 8
SLEEVE BOARDS. Diagrams 7 and 8

3

Either a single or a double board ; if double, it should be a fixed, and not a folding board, as the latter is not firm enough for pressing tailor-made garments.

Sleeve boards can be obtained, the price for a single one being from 1s. 6d., according to the size, and for a double one, from 3s. 9d. Only a small size is needed for ladies' tailoring.

SKIRT BOARD

This is used for tacking and for pressing the seams of skirts, etc.; it can be had for about 4s. 6d.

A SEWING MACHINE (lockstitch)

A DRESS STAND

A stand, padded to about nine inches below the waist-line, is the most useful for fitting on and moulding the bodice or coat.

A dress stand can be purchased in stock sizes, or made to order from a well-fitting bodice, from about 15s. and 25s. respectively.

II. MATERIALS REQUIRED FOR TAILORING

CLOTH, TWEED, OR SERGE
SUITABLE LININGS
FRENCH CANVAS

This canvas (string colour) is used for interlining the fronts of coats, waistcoats, collars, revers, flaps of pockets, etc., to give them the necessary firmness.

It can be had in two thicknesses—the finer make is the more suitable for ladies' tailoring.

It can be obtained from any good tailor's trimming shop, at 6d. per yard.

There is also a white canvas made, for interlining white coats, etc.

LINEN (black or white)

This is used as an interlining for strengthening buttonholes, and for placing under buttons, to strengthen the openings and the corners of pockets, to form a bridle to prevent the crease edge of the revers from stretching out of shape, to give firmness to the cuff or the bottom of sleeves ; also as an interlining to the hem of skirts requiring extra firmness, and to be placed under any part of the garment which is to be ornamented with machine stitching, so that the stitches may be raised to the surface.

The linen should be of a *firm* make, but not heavy or stiff. It can be had from any good draper's, and costs from about 8d. per yard.

TACKING COTTON

This can be bought in large reels of 1,000 yards for 2¾d. and 3¾d., according to the thickness.

So much tacking is necessary in good tailoring that it is extravagant to use good sewing cotton for it.

MACHINE SILK

Quarter-ounce reels of coloured silks are best, as they can be had in different numbers, price 4½d. per reel. One-ounce reels of black silk are the most economical, and cost from about 1s. 4½d. per reel.

BUTTONHOLE TWIST

This is sold by the yard or in penny reels. The twist on the reels is only made in one thickness, but that sold by the yard is of various thicknesses, and costs from a penny a yard, according to size.

LINEN THREAD

This thread is used (twisted and waxed) in the working of tailor's buttonholes, and it should match the twist in colour as nearly as possible.

It is sold in skeins, and can be had at any good tailor's trimming shop.

III. STITCHES USED IN TAILORING

TACKING AND BASTING

Tacking is a stitch made by passing the needle and cotton in and out of the material in a horizontal direction, taking up a small piece of material, and passing over a much larger piece, forming a longer stitch on the right side.

It is used for fixing the seams of garments together so that they may be easily and correctly stitched ; if extra firmness is necessary, an occasional backstitch can be made.

For tacking seams of bodices together for trying on, the stitches should be made smaller, taking up the same amount of material as has been passed over.

Cotton of a contrasting colour is best for tacking, as it is easily distinguished, and the tacked line can be followed in the stitching, ensuring a straight line to the seam.

Basting is also used for holding two materials together, but this stitch is more suitable for fixing in linings, etc., or where large spaces have to be covered with the stitch.

Both tacking and basting must always be done with the materials lying flat on the table, or on a board, *not over the hand,* or the upper side will be puckered.

TAILOR TACKING

This is the tailor's method of tracing the line of the seams, or any other part of the garment (which has already been outlined in tailor's chalk on the *first* half), *through* to the *second* half. If carefully done, the two halves will be found to match exactly.

To tailor tack a seam, place the two halves of the garment flat on the table—*exactly* one over the other—the one which has been marked with chalk for the seams uppermost.

Thread a needle with a long, double length of tacking cotton, but do not make a knot at the end. Tack exactly on the chalk line *right through* the two materials (thus sewing them together), take up only a small amount of material on the needle, leave a *long, loose* stitch; repeat these alternate *small* and *long, loose* stitches all along the chalked line.

When this has been done, draw the two pieces of material slightly apart, and cut the stitches between them, but without drawing any of the threads out of either of the two pieces of the material.

The scissors to cut these stitches *must* be sharp; *short* scissors are more convenient than long ones, and there is less risk of snipping the material with them

STITCHING AND MACHINE STITCHING

These are used for joining seams, ornamental work, etc.

FELLING

Felling is a stitch used by tailors in place of hemming (as it does not show so much, and is less likely to pucker), for putting linings into coats, sewing on collars, facing revers, etc. The work is held in exactly the opposite direction to that in which it is in hemming, and the stitch is shorter and straighter. Fine silk should be used for felling.

OVERSEWING

This stitch is used for sewing over the raw edges of buttonholes, etc. (before working them), when the material is one likely to fray, such as serge.

PADDING

In tailoring, padding is a stitch used in collars and revers of coats to make them roll.

It is done with rather fine silk to match the cloth.

Instructions for working this stitch will be given in a lesson on the making of a coat-collar and revers.

BUTTONHOLE STITCH

Tailor's buttonholes are worked in exactly the opposite direction to a dressmaker's—*i.e.* from right to left, instead of from left to right. The method of preparing and working tailor's buttonholes will be given in a future lesson.

STOATING AND RANTERING

These stitches are used for invisible joins in cloth.

Stoating is done by placing the two pieces of material to be joined flat on a board or table, with the wrong side uppermost—the *edges* having been cut perfectly even that they may exactly meet. Use a length of fine silk to match the cloth, and a fine needle; draw the two raw edges together by working over and over through half the thickness of the cloth; this should form a row of straight stitches across the join, on the wrong side (which is uppermost), and *no* stitches should show on the under or right side. The stitches should be made rather close together.

N.B. It is a good plan to make chalk marks *across* the two raw edges, to ensure their being kept evenly together whilst working, so that neither side is puckered.

RANTERING

The two edges of the cloth which are to be joined should be put together, the *right* side of each piece facing, and level, as for a seam. Neatly backstitch them together by hand, as close to the edges as possible. This stitching should never be done *by machine*, as the line of stitches would be too straight and the join more visible.

The work must now be turned right over, so that the *wrong* side of each piece will be facing the other.

Roll the edge firmly with the thumb and first finger of the left hand, to get the stitches as near the surface as possible, and, whilst holding it firmly in this position, pass a *fine* needle (threaded with *fine* silk to match the cloth) in a slanting direction, just under the surface of the cloth, from one rolled edge to the other; bring the needle out on the right side, and in working the next stitch put it back again in the *same* place at which it was brought out, as *no* stitch must appear on the right side.

Rantering is worked from right to left; it should form a darn of slanting, invisible stitches, joining the two *rolled* edges together.

The seam must be constantly rolled whilst working, to get the stitches as near as possible to the surface. When the work is finished open out the seam, and slightly fray the surface of the cloth on the right side with the point of the needle across the join; damp and press the work *well* on the wrong side.

A join properly rantered is all but invisible.

FINE DRAWING

This stitch is used for the invisible repairing of rents and accidental cuts in cloth. If the rent is a long one, it is a good plan to tack it right side uppermost (the raw edges *close* together) on to a piece of stiff, smooth paper or American cloth, and to make chalk lines *across* the two edges of the rent, or cut, as a guide to keep them level while the work is being done.

The first practical lesson in tailoring will be given in Part 2 of EVERY WOMAN'S ENCYCLOPÆDIA

5

PRACTICAL MILLINERY

By Mrs. ERIC PRITCHARD

The Difficult Art of Making Hat-frames—The Head Band and the Early Stages of the Brim—How to Shape the Brim—The Crown Must be Made Separately

THE difficulty of constructing the framework of headgear without long training and experience cannot be denied, but, like everything else, it can be overcome if we really make up our minds to begin at the beginning and to learn the scientific principles on which this art depends.

No millinery is easy, and to make shapes in wire or spartra requires mathematical precision and accuracy to ensure success.

Spartra is the better material, and can be purchased from any draper at 1s. the sheet. To begin the undertaking, buy one sheet of spartra, 1s. ; one ring of silk wire, 3d. ; and a pair of millinery nippers, which cost 1s. 4½d.

DIRECTIONS

20 Inches

To form the head band. Cut off 22 inches of wire, and make an accurate circle 20 inches in circumference —that is to say, allow 2 inches for overlapping. Give the silk on wire one stitch through, then bind the thread round until the wire is firm.

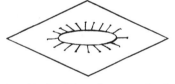

Place this ring flat on the centre of a sheet of spartra, pin it down firmly, then pencilmark round to obtain head mark.

Remove wire, and cut out circle three-quarters of an inch within the head mark.

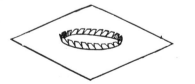

Snip round and turn back to head mark, thus forming a castellated ridge.

Replace head wire on head mark, and firmly buttonhole-stitch all round to prevent stretching of crown.

1 inch

SPARTRA . ——— .

22 Inches

Cut a strip of spartra 1 inch wide by 22 inches long (the two extra inches are allowed for turning).

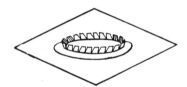

Sew this band firmly to snips. This forms the head band.

Band sewn on to snips.

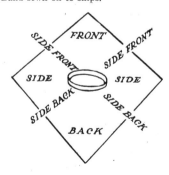

SIDE FRONT   FRONT   SIDE FRONT

SIDE   SIDE

SIDE BACK   SIDE BACK

BACK

To form the brim, one angle of the sheet of spartra must be selected as the front of the hat, and then pencilled into eight equal parts, as shown in sketch.

To cut the brim, take the tape measure and measure off 6 inches along the back line, and 5¼ along the front line, 7½ along the side

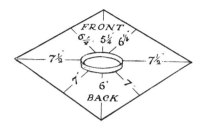

lines, and 6¼ along front side lines, and 7 inches along back side lines. Cut round these marks so as to form an even oval.

Be very careful to get your edge perfectly straight all around. This is by no means an easy task. The edge of brims in amateur millinery—and, indeed, often among experts—leaves much to be desired in this respect, and may frequently be described as " bumpy."

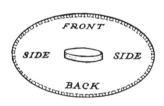

Diagram showing double wire round edge of brim buttonholed together, then stitched on to edge of brim with a long stitch on the top and a short stitch through.

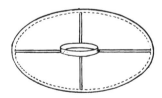

The brim has now to be supported by wires to prevent drooping. In the shape given a wire support is required at front, back, and sides, as illustrated ; some shapes require more, others fewer, supports. In the case of small hats, or tiny mushroom shapes, supports are seldom required, and in all cases they must be used with discretion, as they add to the weight of a hat. On the other hand, an extra support must be used when a tilt or a droop on one side is desired. It is advisable to carry these supports right up the head. They are stitched on in the same way as the wire round the brim.

Get a piece of muslin, cut on the cross, ¾ inch wide, and bind over edge of wires and supports to prevent the wire from

SPARTRA. — .
26 Inches

cutting through. For binding supports, lay the muslin on flatly and stitch through.

We now start the all-important crown ; this has to be made quite separately.

Cut band of spartra 26 inches long by 3½ inches high, join into a round— the circumference being, when finished, 24 inches.

24 Inches.

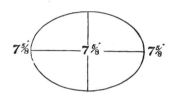

For top piece of crown, cut a round of spartra and fit it on the top. The measurements for crown to fit on to the band would be 7⅝ by 7⅝.

Wire round firmly, and sew on to band as illustrated, then cover the stitches with a binding of muslin. The bottom of the band is also wired.

This hat—in the two separate pieces, namely, the crown and the brim—is not joined together until both are covered separately with the chosen material.

Sketch of hat as it should look when covered with the material.

The next article, in Part 2 of EVERY WOMAN'S ENCYCLOPÆDIA, will deal with the *covering* of shapes, and the cutting and stretching of fabrics. The shape is illustrated *covered*, but, as explained, the crown and brim should not be joined together until they are carefully finished *separately*.

7

PRACTICAL ADVICE ON THE CHOICE OF FURS

By The Hon. Mrs. FITZROY STEWART

No. 1.—SABLES

Where Sable Come From—Secrets of the Fur Trade—Frauds, and How to Detect them "Shaded" Skins—Care of Sables—Value of Sable

Furs, lace, and pearls are the articles of dress most prized by the modern Englishwoman. They can be worn by young girls, for whom rich ornaments are out of place ; they may be used in mourning ; and they are favoured by those whose fine taste shrinks from a display of jewels or of splendid materials.

THE SABLE'S HOME

Sable is one of the most beautiful of furs. It was not known in Europe until long after ermine had been discovered. The sable had its home in the north-east of Asia, and the Russians are said to have conquered Siberia so as to acquire a right to these fur-producing districts. The sable is a native of Siberia, and is found in its coldest regions, at least wherever there are forests of enough density, and the progress of discovery in the north-eastern parts of Siberia has been much indebted to the expeditions of hardy and daring sable hunters.

These men explore new regions at the worst seasons of the year, and spend dreary months at a great distance from human abodes. They have many a hard day in the snow before they catch this small but precious creature, whose tracks can hardly be seen in the wide snow wastes.

The sable is taken in traps, which are a kind of pitfall, as the greatest care must be used to avoid injury to the fur. In some cases it is tracked through the snow to its hole, and caught by placing a net over the entrance.

The sable is wary game, and by no means easily captured. The little animal makes its nest in a hollow tree, or else by burrowing in the ground, and in either case lines its lair with soft layers of moss, grass, or leafage. From this it issues to prey on smaller creatures, and it is so agile that it can catch birds in the branches of trees.

Although the sable inhabits the Arctic regions, it does not, like many Arctic animals, change to white in the winter, for, as it lives mostly amongst dark branches, white would be fatally conspicuous.

Sable is a species of marten, and so nearly allied to the common marten that it is hard to state specific distinctions. There is, however, one marked difference—namely, that the sable's feet are covered with fur, even to the soles, and that its tail is more bushy than that of the marten. It is about the same size as the marten, the length of its body averaging twelve inches, and that of its tail about seven or eight inches. These tails are valuable as a decorative feature on muffs.

WHERE THE FINEST SABLE COMES FROM

Russian and Canadian sables bear the finest fur in the world. The over-hair is most lustrous, the wool close and soft, and the skin very fine and pliable. The fur is brown in colour, but varies in shades and texture with the different species of animal. Russian sable is by far the most valuable, and the finest skins come from the forests of Yakutsk in Siberia.

According to Russian law they are tribute to the Crown, and are therefore not marketable. But the present Emperor, like the two who preceded him, waives this right, and the finest sables all come to the London market, where Russian jobbers bid for them, and take a certain number of skins back for sale at retail prices in St. Petersburg. The best skins are of an ashen brown shade, merging into a dim black towards the back, and the blackest are by far the most valuable. A ready market for this choice fur is also found in New York and Paris.

THE PRICE OF SABLES

Sable skins of the finest quality are worth at retail price in London from £70 to £100 apiece. And even more may be given if the customer desires the furrier to exercise the right, in accordance with trade custom, of paying ten per cent above market rates in order to ransack not only his own stocks, but all the skins in London, so that he may choose the darkest colour in which it is possible to match the number of skins needed. And the small size of the skins greatly increases the cost of a garment.

A sable coat collar is often priced at from £200 to £250 ; a large muff formed of eight skins, each skin worth £70, will fetch £560 ; a long coat of average Russian sable is worth from £1,500 ; and one made of specially fine skins may cost £3,000. Sable coats made in Russia are often of historic value, especially what are known as "shubes," the long, large coats that are worn for sledge journeys.

One of these, made of black sable, was presented to an English peer by a former Emperor of Russia, and has been handed down as an heirloom in that nobleman's family. This cloak is of dark blue cloth lined with sable, and a piece of the same fur a quarter of a yard deep borders the edge of this costly mantle.

There are, of course, cheaper kinds of sable, such as the Hudson Bay variety, obtained from the Canadian market. This fur is also thick and soft, and its colour is warm brown, with a yellowish tinge at the side, and a

8

darker tint along the back. The skins range from £15 up to £40, which latter is about half the price of the best Russian sable. Then come the lighter Russian sables, that are artificially "shaded" or topped, and which cost from £4 a skin upwards ; and even cheaper are the Kolinski sables, which by nature are bright yellow, but are dyed to resemble Russian sables in colour. For about £80 to £100 a short coat or cape of "shaded" sable may be obtained.

This, although it cannot vie with one made of skins worth £80 apiece, yet looks almost as well as medium quality Russian skins priced at £30 each, and, on the whole, better than the light Russian sables sold in their natural colour at £8 or £10 apiece.

A first-rate authority declares that the price of the best Russian sable has risen at least 75 per cent. during the last few years ; and it bids fair to go higher, as the supply seems to fall short of the demand. In a luxurious age, sable has become a necessity.

SECRETS OF THE FUR TRADE

The fur trade has some interesting secrets. There is a skilful method of working sable and other small skins of the same description. By this means what looks like one large skin can be made out of two or three small ones.

The skins are first carefully matched, and then almost cut to pieces. The bits are afterwards joined again, all the necks put together like one large neck, all the centre parts like one large centre, and, lastly, all the tails are formed

A sable coat   *Henri Manuel*

into one thick tail. When thus joined up the effect is marvellous, and it has all the appearance of one big skin to the uninitiated.

Then the "shading" or "topping" of fur is also an admitted process. "Shading" does not mean that the entire fur is dyed, but that the tips of the hair are lightly brushed over with a dye which gives a darker colour. If expense is an object, there is no

need to avoid "shaded" sables. The skins are adorned, not falsified.

FRAUDS AND HOW TO DETECT THEM

Frauds in the fur trade consist in selling "shaded" skins as natural skins, or selling substitutes under a false name, and such frauds are most often applied to one of the most costly of all furs—the darkest Russian sable. Besides darkening the over-hair, white badger hairs are either gummed in, or drawn through the pelt with a needle, so as to give the effect of the silvery over-hairs, which appear here and there in the finer grades of Russian sable.

An expert has given some simple tests which will enable an amateur to detect the grosser counterfeits. One test is to double the skin over, with the fur outwards, and to look through the ridge of over-hair towards bright sunlight. The tips of the over-hair in both natural and "shaded" skins are darker than the lower part of the hair, so in looking at them in this way one perceives a high-water mark, half way from hide to tip, where the colour suddenly darkens.

ARTIFICIALLY "SHADED" SKINS

In the artificially "shaded" skin this high-water mark is an absolutely straight line, for the dye has been evenly brushed along the surface of the over-hair, and unless the tips are darkened one by one— which is practically impossible—the result must, of course, be uniform. Where the darkness of the tips is natural the mark is, however, broken by a series of curves and lines.

Another test is to pluck out a few of the blackest hairs and dip them into a strong acid. Natural sable hairs will fade to a lighter shade, just as would hair from the human head ; but in the case of any dye now in use it is probable that the acid would not merely fade the tips of the dyed hair, but would bring out a tinge of green or orange-

9

purple. The word "probable" is written with intention, as no test has yet been found which will infallibly reveal dyed sable to the untrained observer.

Fraud, however, is apt to go much further. The skins of mink, hare, squirrel, rabbit, marmot, and musquash are often dyed and substituted for those of sable. In this case the trick is more easy to discover, as there is a palpable difference in texture. If the hairs are blown apart, or if the hand is run up and down the skin, the fraud may be easily detected.

A woman who buys sable ought to insist that the skins sold her should be specifically described as "natural and not dyed," and this statement must be made in writing. A salesman who has no scruple as to a verbal guarantee will refuse to make out a bill in this form, and thereby run the risk of either civil or criminal proceedings.

Good furriers may be found in London whose word is their bond ; and such as these would lose and not gain by unfair proceedings. Furs and the fur trade are now under the ægis of an Act of Parliament.

CARE OF SABLES

Sable needs the most careful treatment. When not in use it should be taken out from time to time, lightly wiped over with a cambric handkerchief, and then either shaken or beaten. A gentle beating is best. A light cane should be used, and, after beating, the fine hairs should be combed lengthways and across—a coarse, three-inch comb is best for this purpose, and is the sort generally used by furriers. If sable has been rained upon it should be hung up to dry in a current of air before it is put away again.

Fire is fatal to fur ; and good skins ought never to be set near it to dry, as is often done by the untaught and careless.

The story goes that a precious sable coat which had got wet was hung on a fire-guard to dry with direful consequences. The fur changed colour after a short time, the hairs came out, and in the end the costly coat was ruined.

Good sable is portable property of much value, and its care in the summer needs some forethought. The best plan is to put one's treasures into the hands of a good furrier who knows his business, and whose cold storage rooms are fitted up with all the latest improvements.

In this case the furs should be duly insured against fire and burglary. But in these days of chilly summers many women prefer to keep their sables always in their own houses. In fact, a smart woman may often be seen wearing her fur on a cool day when driving in a motor in the afternoon, or at a cricket match at Lord's, or at one of the race meetings. But moths mean mischief ; and if good sables are kept at home they must be stored in a zinc-lined box or in a cedar chest for the sake of safety. And if the skins are of great value, or if we have what the furriers call a "mothy" summer, each article should be stored into a linen bag or wrapper, and only taken out as occasion demands.

SABLES AND SABLE SCHEMES

Sable is not always adaptable. As regards colour, it looks its best with some shades of brown, and with white, black, cream, or grey. But with red, green, yellow, bright blue, or bright violet it becomes difficult. And it does not mix well with other furs—sealskin is the only exception. Sable suits most good complexions, but it favours a woman with dark hair and brunette colouring.

This series of articles will be continued in Part 2 of Every Woman's Encyclopædia.

COLOUR AND CLOTHES

Wear Colours which are Becoming, not necessarily those which are Fashionable—The Difficulties of Dressing the Woman with Auburn Hair—Look to Nature for Colour Schemes—England is a Dull Country, therefore be Cheerful in your Dress

ONCE when cross-questioned by a woman as to the ingredients which he used in mixing his colours, a famous artist comprehensively replied that he mixed them with brains. Similarly, success in clothes is achieved only if the colours are not merely mixed but applied with brains.

In the choice of colours, as in all matters connected with clothes, individuality in women should be strongly encouraged. That one colour should be more fashionable than another is in itself an absurdity. It might almost as well be asserted that a special kind of complexion or a particular shape of face should be worn to the exclusion of all others.

The only colour that has any right to be fashionable is the colour that happens to suit the wearer, and nothing is more foolish than for every woman, dark or fair, pale or ruddy, fat or thin, to imagine that, because

there happens to be an epidemic of mustard-yellow or peacock-green, she must, therefore, clothe herself in aggressive tints that fight all day long with her hair and her complexion. That a colour is essentially and undoubtedly becoming should be its first passport to our good graces.

THE DIFFICULTIES OF AUBURN HAIR

The woman who gaily crowns a mass of auburn locks with a biscuit-coloured hat garlanded with bright pink roses—and, strange though it may seem, red-haired people have often a passion for pink and crimson—does not realise that her hair, beautiful as it is in itself, is a subject which must be studied very carefully in its relation to her hats.

Let her wear a large picture shape in soft black crinoline, with a brim which will cast mysterious shadows over hair and brow. This will make a delightful contrast to the vivid locks beneath. Furthermore, let her drape the crown of her hat with masses of black tulle, and group on one side of it three or four long black ostrich feathers. The whole effect will be delightful, and, if she will refrain from the introduction even of a white osprey or a pale cream rose, it shall be counted to her for further righteousness.

Brilliant auburn hair, however, even at the present time, is very rare, unless—low let it be spoken—it is assisted liberally with henna. The woman who possesses such hair, however, should first choose black, but there are soft shades of grey and tender blues in which she may also revel.

White garments are fairly safe, but all tones of rose, pink, crimson, bright violet, or vivid green should carefully be avoided.

FLOWER SCHEMES

The modern élégante, seeking inspiration for the colour of her gowns, might do worse than adopt a flower scheme for her afternoon frocks. Let her take some decorative blossom—for example, the purple iris—and work out a complete toilette. The gown can be carried out in shades of pale lilac and deep violet, and a hint of pearl grey suggested in the *frou frou* of a satin petticoat. Filmy laces, ivory-white, can deck the throat and wrists, and a pale lilac hat can be worn, trimmed only with dark violet velvet iris. For a brunette the varying tones of wallflowers are excellent in inspiring a becoming day or evening gown. Rich browns, with here and there a fleck of orange or bright yellow, will be found harmonious and becoming, while to complete the realism, a knot of soft grey-green should not be omitted, for the leaves and stalks of wallflowers play an important part in the charm of this richly perfumed plant.

The Frenchwoman, to whom nothing connected with the subtlety of dress is unimportant, has long ago adopted the plan of using a perfume suitable to the costume. When she dons a heliotrope-coloured dress, then does she use the sweet "cherry-pie" scent; when in white, lily blossom perfume; with dark violet, violette de parme is used; and so on throughout the gamut of colour and perfume.

The tall, fair woman might find inspiration in the lily of the valley, with its fresh, cool contrast of white and green, or in the delicate pink of the briar rose. In the spring-time, the pale gold of the laburnum commends itself to dark and fair alike; the deep purple of the wood violet or the delicate mauve of the lilac blossom, which always is emphasised and rendered more attractive by those touches of leaf-green which Nature herself indicates as the one means of bringing into harmony all the tints of all the flowers that grow.

For autumn gowns, again, what finer inspiration is there for modiste or milliner alike than the brilliant crimson and the russet browns of the woodland foliage; than all the wonderful gradations of gold and bronze which shine out upon us from the October trees and from the creepers which fling their gorgeous mantles far and wide? In fur-trimmed velvets there are no colours lovelier than those which are borrowed from the autumn leaves.

THE VALUE OF CONTRAST

Under our grey English skies flashes of bright colour come as a welcome relief, and should do much to lighten the gloom of dark November days.

As a nation we are a little too much inclined to be afraid of vivid tints. We take our pleasures sadly, and are disposed to echo in our garments the dull, dark tones which too often seem part and parcel of our English atmosphere.

To break away from this tradition is to benefit our fellow-creatures, and the woman who is hesitating between Quaker-grey and a brilliant shade of crimson for a winter walking-gown, will do well to choose the latter, for she will be doing something towards lightening the dulness of our streets.

NATURE SCHEMES

Skies at sunrise and sunset give many an inspiration for day-gowns in delicate tones of pink and grey, and for evening frocks too, where misty veilings of tulle and chiffon are draped so that a deeper tone shines out from an under-robe of satin.

Suggestions also may be found of crimson, gold, or purple fading into lilac, of ruby melting into palest sapphire; vague evanescent colourings as fugitive and beautiful as the wide bars of light drawn at sunset across the western sky.

For tea-gowns and for evening frocks there are possibilities in all the wonderful blues and greens of the sea, and those mysterious tints which glitter on the track painted by the moonlight upon the surface of the water, or, again, in the purples which the cloud shadows leave as the sunlight chases them over the hills.

All these colours afford schemes worthy of consideration, especially if we are able to use those many lovely tissues in silver and gold which are interwoven with threads of sea-green and of sapphire blue. These veilings can be draped again with ivory-white silk net, so fine as to be visible only in its softening effect upon the colouring of the other fabrics.

WHITE AND ITS POSSIBILITIES

Although, technically speaking, white implies an absence of colour, many delightful possibilities are afforded by its lovely suggestions of pearl and snow and ivory. The bride looks her best in her white wedding-gown.

The following are good firms for supplying materials mentioned in this Section Messrs. Burberry's (Weatherproof Coats), Dean's Rag Book Co., Ltd. (Publishers), Henan-Gingell Shoe Co., Ltd. (Footwear), Horrockses' (Longcloths and Sheetings), Kleinert Depot (Hose Supporters), Dr. Lahmann (Cottonwool Underwear), London Glove Co. (Gloves), Lutas Leathley & Co. (Dress Fabrics), Sandow's Corset Co. (Corsets).

F

WOMAN'S DRESS

Conducted by the Editress of "Fashions for All"

In this important section of EVERY WOMAN'S ENCYCLOPÆDIA every aspect of dress will be dealt with by practical and experienced writers. The history of dress from earliest times will be told, and practical and useful information will be given in :

Home Dressmaking		Millinery
How to Cut Patterns	*Home Tailoring*	*Lessons in Hat Trimming*
Methods of Self-measure-	*Representative Fashions*	*How to Make a Shape*
ment	*Fancy Dress*	*How to Curl Feathers*
Colour Contrasts	*Alteration of Clothes, etc.*	*Flowers, Hat-pins, Colours, etc.*
Boots and Shoes	**Furs**	**Gloves**
Choice	*Choice*	*Choice*
How to Keep in Good Condition	*How to Preserve, etc.*	*Cleaning, etc.*
How to Soften Leather, etc.	*How to Detect Frauds*	**Jewellery, etc.**

PRACTICAL ADVICE ON THE CHOICE OF FURS

By The Hon. Mrs. FITZROY STEWART

Continued from page 78, Part 1

No. 2.—FOX

The Characteristics and Markings of the Various Species of Fox—the Price and Value cf Different Furs—The Fur Market and the Fur Trade

AMONG the most precious of furs must be reckoned those of the silver and blue fox. The silver, or, as it is sometimes called, black, fox, is found in Alaska, Columbia, and the Hudson Bay Territory. The best skins come from Labrador, and many of the finest find their way into the London market.

The silver fox has black legs, a thick, bushy tail, and is smaller than its European relations. Its feet are peculiar. Richardson says : " The black and silver foxes have the soles of their feet thickly covered with wool in the winter ; no callous spots are then visible."

Silver Fox

Silver fox fur is rare, but for softness and firmness it has no equal.

As regards colour, it is a beautiful rich, glossy black, and the longer and outer hairs are silvery white. This contrast in shade is most attractive. The neck of the silver fox is black, and this black fur extends behind the shoulders and down the back, sometimes almost to the quarters.

A single skin of fine silver fox is worth £150, and one of great beauty will fetch at least £200. A muff of the best silver fox

fur would cost £150, and a long stole about £300 ; indeed, the price of the latter might run even to £600 or £700.

Silver fox is a fur which seems to harmonise with everything, and this, no doubt, is one of the reasons for its popularity among Parisians.

Black Fox

Natural black fox of the best quality is a fur of almost fabulous value. A good black skin, with only the characteristic white tip at the end of the tail, will fetch a fancy price in the fur markets.

This precious fur is much worn by the Russian nobility, and of late years the best skins have been sold less freely in London and Paris than in St. Petersburg—that is, if any fur can be said to sell " freely " at prices ranging for a single skin from £300 to £800. This latter price is said by a leading expert to have been given for one skin of extreme beauty and blackness. The late Emperor Alexander II. of Russia wore, when in London, a coat made of the necks of black fox, which was then valued at £3,500. And the price of fur has risen so much of late years that a coat which contained the same number of skins of a like quality would now be worth £12,000. The finest black fox fur has become a rarity. There are but two or three quite black skins in a whole year's collection, and some immense districts do not produce one such skin during an entire winter. In fact, the best black and silver fox furs are so costly that most of us wish in vain for luck such as befell Nansen, the famous explorer.

Once, when encamped in the Arctic regions, he laid wait for foxes which had stolen hams from his stores, and was fortunate enough to bring to his gun a number of the true silver foxes. Their fur was worth almost its weight in gold, and for such skins as these skilled trappers had searched in vain under conditions of the greatest hardship.

Blue Fox

Blue fox—so-called—is brownish grey in colour, or, in the best specimens, deep slate. The blue fox is smaller than the silver variety, and has a thick, bushy tail, and black legs, which are longer than those of foxes found in Europe. The fur is of high price and a most delicate beauty. A muff of the finest blue fox would cost from £40, and a stole from £50 to £80.

This rare animal is found in Greenland, the Pribylov Islands, and the Hudson Bay Territory. Blue fox was the favourite fur of Catherine de Medici, and at that time one of the most highly prized furs in existence. It does not, as some writers say, turn white in the winter. It always remains a blue fox.

Several other members of the fox family produce fur which is useful and decorative. There is the Arctic, or white, fox, the red fox, the grey fox, and an iron-yellow fox found in Tartary. The skin of the latter is known in the trade as Cossack fur. Japan sends 60,000 foxes a year to the London market. These, however, are small, and used chiefly for collars and trimmings.

The Arctic Fox

The Arctic fox is a small creature only two feet in length, and its coat, brownish in summer, becomes pure white as winter approaches. The white fox breeds on the sea-coast, and lives chiefly within the Arctic circle. The best and whitest skins come from the shores of Labrador. This species of fox is said to be best for dyeing purposes, as its skin is less liable to change in colour after the process.

White fox fur seems to be always in high favour. It is soft, fluffy, and becoming, but looks its best when worn by a blonde, or by a young, fresh girl. This snow-white fur is not suitable for wear under the grey skies and in the smoke and fogs of London.

Arctic fox fur frequently needs cleaning, but this can be done at small expense, as the stitches need not be unpicked nor the skins treated in revolving drums full of hot sand and sawdust of a special wood — a method used by furriers when furs need more than a superficial treatment.

A white fox muff costs about £1, and a stole perhaps £20; but the price, of course, depends upon the colour and quality.

The cross fox is found in Norway, but the best skins come from the Labrador district.

The cross fox is of the same species as the red fox, but its colouring is different. Like the blue fox it is small in size, about two feet long. Its legs and ears are black, and its tail, which is thick and bushy, has a white tip. Its coat is marked with yellow streaks, and a longitudinal dark line runs down the centre of the back. This forms a sort of cross, and explains the fox's name. This fur, if dyed, makes a good imitation

Silver fox muff and stole
Copyright International Fur Store

of silver fox. The skins cost £10 each, and make good boas and muffs. A boa might cost £15, a muff £20, and a long stole about £40.

The American Fox

The American fox is red like its British relation. Its fur, however, is not used much in this country.

The grey fox comes from Virginia and other southern states, and is never found north of Maine. The fur is not of much value, but makes up into rugs and footbags. The Chinese fox is of a pale yellow colour. The skins are cheap, but not attractive.

The Fox: Its Habits, etc.

Foxes are a group of animals that belong to the dog family. They average from two to four feet in length, and are characterised by their slight build, long, thick tails, short legs, and long ears. The pupil of the eye is elliptical when contracted, and not circular, as in dogs, wolves, and jackals. They indulge in a wide range of nutriment. Their food includes animals of the size of

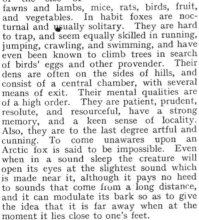

Arctic fox in winter coat
Photo by W. S. Berridge, F.Z.S.

fawns and lambs, mice, rats, birds, fruit, and vegetables. In habit foxes are nocturnal and usually solitary. They are hard to trap, and seem equally skilled in running, jumping, crawling, and swimming, and have even been known to climb trees in search of birds' eggs and other provender. Their dens are often on the sides of hills, and consist of a central chamber, with several means of exit. Their mental qualities are of a high order. They are patient, prudent, resolute, and resourceful, have a strong memory, and a keen sense of locality. Also, they are to the last degree artful and cunning. To come unawares upon an Arctic fox is said to be impossible. Even when in a sound sleep the creature will open its eyes at the slightest sound which is made near it, although it pays no heed to sounds that come from a long distance, and it can modulate its bark so as to give the idea that it is far away when at the moment it lies close to one's feet.

The Fur Market

Fallacies exist on the subject of furs as on most other mundane affairs. Many of us imagine that the centre of the fur trade is at Nijni Novgorod, in Russia, and that each season the finest skins find their way from there to the shops of retail furriers in St. Petersburg. But this is not the case.

The world's prime market for furs is London. The sable and silver fox sold in St. Petersburg, the sealskin and beaver sold

in Toronto, and the chinchilla on view at Lima have usually passed through the London market, and then made the journey back to Russia, Peru, and Canada.

London, moreover, is the best place in which to buy furs ; the buying of furs in Norway, at Carlsbad, or at Monte Carlo is not so economical as some women seem to imagine.

Again, the stock of furs held in London is much larger than elsewhere ; in London the retail furrier can match the finest skins that may be required by an exacting customer.

The great London houses have a world-wide trade. They supply fur to the Courts of Europe, and have provided most of the Coronation robes that have been worn during the last few generations. Even the black fox skins for the wondrous coat that belonged to the late Emperor of Russia were supplied, and the coat itself made, by a London furrier, although the foxes had been trapped in the Tsar's own dominions.

Few persons have any idea of the magnitude of the fur trade. The lists of furs sold at public auction in London showed that during one year the Hudson Bay Company sold 670 skins of silver, 3,165 of cross, and 4,898 of white foxes. These, however, are small quantities when compared with the vast store of furs imported by private enterprise from the United States, Canada, and other British provinces in North America. A list of the above states that in one year there came to our market 1,503 skins of silver fox, 4,458 of blue fox, 5,460 of cross fox, 47,725 of grey fox, and no fewer than 77,705 of the white Arctic fox.

As a rule, the nearer an animal lives to the Equator the more brilliant will be the colour of its fur. Animals that live in woods and forests give finer fur than those which live on open prairies. Sea air coarsens and thickens fur ; hence sables trapped inland have finer coats than sables from Kamtchatka.

Most furs can be copied with fair success, but silver fox stands almost alone in that it is above imitation. Its great price sets it apart, as no one would give £150 or more for a single skin unless she were certain of the genuine article.

White fox, however, can be easily copied. For this purpose the skins of white hares are used, and the black fox fur of everyday life is made from the skins of white foxes or red foxes, dyed to the required colour. These, however, must not be termed frauds, as they are confessed imitations.

This series will be continued.

PRACTICAL MILLINERY

By MRS. ERIC PRITCHARD

Continued from page 76, Part 1

How to Cover the Shape—Cutting the Material—Stretching and Fitting the Cloth over the Brim—
Slipstitching the Edges—Joining the Crown to the Brim

THE last article dealt entirely with the elementary details of shape making, and left the spartra shape wired ready for covering. This process must now be carefully followed. For the autumn season cloth may be taken as the most seasonable and most popular fabric, with the exception of "mirroir" velvet. The latter material, however, is much more costly and difficult to manipulate. A thin, smooth cloth should be chosen, and it is unwise to give less than 3s.

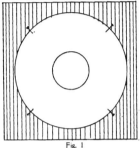

Fig. 1

11d. a yard (double width), three-quarters of a yard being sufficient.

Place the spartra shape on a square of the cloth, which should be sufficiently large to allow for turning over the brim. Placing the corner of the cloth to the front, mark its position on the spartra shape (see sketch). The

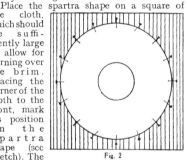

Fig. 2

right side of the material must face the brim, as this piece of cloth is intended, after the necessary fitting has been completed, for the top of the brim. The necessary fitting is carried out as follows :

Pin flatly round the edge, and avoid using many or coarse pins, as they are apt to mark the cloth.

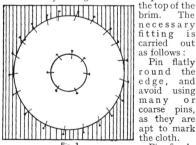

Fig. 3

Pin firmly round the head marks. These operations are clearly shown in the illustrations, which should be closely followed.

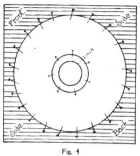

Fig. 4

Cut circle one inch within the head mark.

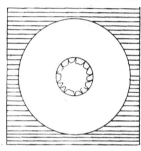

Fig. 5

Snip up as far as the head marks, being very careful not to cut beyond. Then remove the pins.

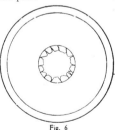

Fig. 6

Mark the front, back, and sides with pins or pencil marks, then cut the cloth round the edge of the brim, not forgetting to leave one inch for turning. Then remove the pins, and take the cloth off the brim.

The cloth should now be replaced on the top of the brim, placing the front, sides, and back marks in their proper positions. The right side of the material must be outside, and the snips will then fit all round on to the side band.

Fig. 7

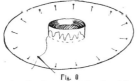

Fig. 0

Sew snips firmly round the head band.

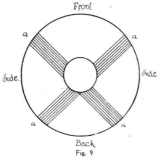

Fig. 9

The difficult task of stretching and fitting the cloth over the brim is now commenced. The material must always be pulled on the straight grain, so that the point of the material lies in *front* (sketch 1), the straight grain will then be at the points (*a*) illustrated in the accompanying sketch.

When the material has been sufficiently stretched on the straight, it can then be stretched on the cross, *i.e.*, at the front, back, and sides.

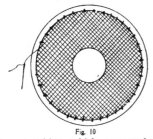

Fig. 10

After stretching, which may make the brim appear uneven, turn over the half-inch

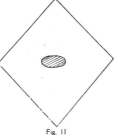

Fig. 11

of cloth which is beyond the brim on to the under-brim, and pin firmly, then sew (as illustrated), being very careful to pick up one thread only of the spartra, to prevent the stitches coming through on the top of the brim.

The top brim being now complete, we take the point of the remaining material and place it on to the front of the under-brim exactly in the same way as in Direction figure 1, and carry out Direction figures 2, 3, 4, and 5, the only difference being that the right side of the material must, of course, be on the outside, and the pins must not be removed after carrying out Direction figure 5.

Fig. 12

Pull and pin the cloth, first on the straight and then on the cross, in the same way as directed for the top of the brim ; and it may at this point be found that an alteration in the head pins will improve the fit. Now sew the snips firmly inside the head, cut the cloth half an inch larger than the brim, and turn it in to meet the edge of the cloth at the top of the brim, pinning it ready for slip-stitching.

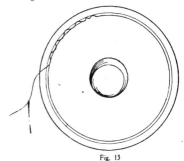

Fig. 13

Slipstitching is one of the most important items in practical millinery, and it is usually found advisable to practise on bandeaux before attempting the edge of a cloth or velvet hat.

The needle must be taken through the piece of material turned over from the top brim, being very careful not to take the stitch through the spartra. Pull the cotton through the back of the under-brim edge, then back again to the top, and pull the edge together.

There are several ways of finishing the edge, such as binding it with a plain or gauged piece of velvet or cloth ; or the rouleau, which is made by working a piece of wire in at each edge, thus forming a neat piping on each side.

16

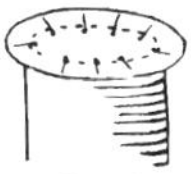

Fig. 14

For the crown of the hat, which should now be taken, cut a circle of the cloth large enough to fit over the top, with an inch beyond for turning, and then pin firmly on.

Turn over the surplus, and sew the edge on to the side band. Then remove the pins.

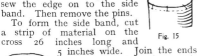

To form the side band, cut a strip of material on the cross 26 inches long and

Fig. 15

5 inches wide. Join the ends so that the circumference is 24 inches, the necessary size to fit the spartra shape.

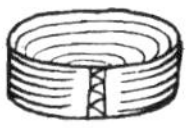

Fig. 16

Place over the spartra. This allows three-quarters of an inch for turnings top and bottom of the band of a 3½-inch-high crown. Then slipstitch the edges together at the top

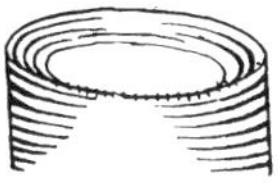

Fig. 17

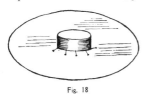

Fig. 18

Pin the crown firmly in the centre of the hat, so that the join in the side band is where it will be hidden by the trimming, and slipstitch again on to the brim.

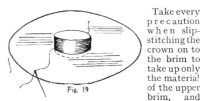

Fig. 19

Take every precaution when slip-stitching the crown on to the brim to take up only the material of the upper brim, and not the spartra (as illustrated).

The pattern shape, which is now almost flat, can be quite successfully covered without putting any pleats in the brim to make it set well ; but for a mushroom shape it is necessary to put pleats in the under-brim to ensure accurate fitting. These are cut down the centre, and one side is made to lap over the other until the fullness has all disappeared (as illustrated).

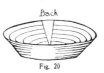

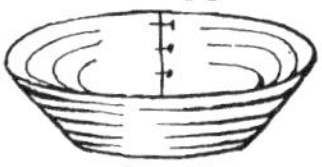

Back

Fig. 20

Slipstitch the cut pleats down the join. Sew as neatly as possible.

The top of the brim hardly ever requires a pleat, as it can be stretched over the shape until the fullness is all pulled away.

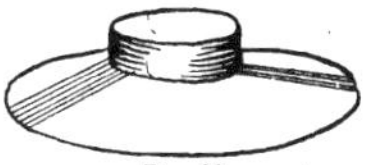

Fig. 21

Fig. 22

The last sketch (No. 22) shows the model hat when finished and ready for trimming, which process will be the subject of the next article. *To be continued.*

PRACTICAL LESSONS IN DRESSMAKING

Continued from page 71, Part 1

By M. PRINCE BROWNE

Examiner in Dressmaking, Tailoring, French Pattern Modelling, Plain Needlework, and Millinery of the Teachers in Training at the University College of South Wales and Monmouthshire, Cardiff ; the London Higher Technical Examination Centres, etc. ; First Class Diploma for Tailoring ; Diploma of Honour for Dressmaking ; Diploma of Merit of the Highest Order for Teaching ; Silver Medallist, London Exhibition, 1900 ; Silver Medal, Franco-British Exhibition, 1908 ; Author of " Up-to-Date Dresscutting and Drafting," also " The Practical Work of Dressmaking and Tailoring."

SECOND LESSON

Fastenings—Bones—Prussian Binding—Lute Ribbon—Skirt Binding—Buckram—Stitches Used in Dressmaking—Tacking—Basting—Running—Gathering—Hemming—Stitching—Back-stitching

Patent hooks and *small* metal rings are sometimes used for fastening placket holes, etc.

The rings must be buttonholed round with twist to match the colour of the dress. The *small* rings are sold in boxes of a gross, in black or white, at 4½d. per box. The patent hooks are sold on cards, and they can be purchased by the dozen. Patent press fasteners are also used for placket-holes, blouses, etc., and are sold in black or white on cards of a dozen or more.

Bones

" Whalebone " or " Baleinette," can be used for boning bodices when desired. Real whalebone is, of course, the best, but this is expensive. It costs from 1s. 1½d. per

strip of one and a half yards in length, and about two and a half strips are required for a fully-boned bodice.

" Baleinette " is the best inexpensive substitute—it is sold by the yard at about 2¾d., or in rolls of a dozen yards at about 2s. 6d. This can very well be used for *draped* bodices, as the extra thickness of the Baleinette is not observable under the draping, but for *plain* bodices real bone is necessary.

Horn, steel, and other such substitutes are not advisable, as they cannot be stitched *through* in boning the bodice, and this stitching *through* the bone is absolutely necessary, to ensure the proper shaping of the bodice. Bones already cut in lengths and sold in packets, or bones *ready* " cased," are undesirable for really good work.

17

For boning the *backs* of *evening* bodices, whether fastened with hooks or laces, a *narrow* whalebone should always be used. This can be purchased in strips from 10¾d. each, according to the length.

Prussian Binding

This is used as a "casing" for the bones down the seams of bodices, also for "facing" the sewing on of hooks and eyes, for loops on the bands of skirts (by which to hang them up), and for "facing" raw edges, etc., to make them neat. It can be had in various colours, but either black or white should always be used for bone casings, as they should match the "tight-band" of the bodice and the band of the skirt, which are always either black or white. The price of Prussian binding is a penny a yard, or 10½d. per dozen. There is a cheaper quality, but it is too clumsy for bone casing. The twilled side of the binding is the right side, and should, of course, be placed uppermost.

Lute Ribbon

This is a plain, soft, sarcenet ribbon, and can be had in various widths and in all colours from 1d. a yard, according to the width. It is sometimes used instead of Prussian binding for bone casings in silk, or silk lined, bodices, for facing the sewing on of hooks and eyes, for binding or "facing" round the basques of bodices, binding seams, "facing" the raw edge of the hem of a skirt (when the material is too thick to be turned in), and sometimes for binding the top of a thin skirt, instead of putting it into a band at the waist.

Skirt Braid and Binding

These are used for preserving the edge of walking skirts. The ordinary plain worsted braid can be had in any colour, and costs from ½d. per yard. Another kind is brush braid, but the appearance is not so good, as it makes the skirt look "frayed." Velveteen binding is sometimes used instead of braid to preserve the bottom of a skirt, which it should match in colour, and if the binding is prepared at home, strips of velveteen should be cut *perfectly* on the cross of the width desired (from 1¼ to 3 inches), the strips being neatly joined together.

N.B.—The method of cutting and joining strips of material on the cross is given in the second lesson on tailoring, with diagrams Nos. 9, 10, 11.

Velvet binding or skirt facing can be bought ready cut in black and all colours from 1½d. per yard, or 1s. 5½d. per dozen yards, according to the width.

Buckram

Buckram is only necessary if the bodice is to be made with a stiff "stand" collar. There are several kinds, but the best is not a heavy make (it is yellowish and waxy-looking, and it is *not rolled*, but folded double, and two collars can be cut from the width). A small quantity is all that is necessary, as a quarter of a yard is sufficient to cut about six collars. It costs 10½d. per yard.

Stitches Used in Dressmaking

Tacking	Hemming	Sewing
Basting	Stitching	Overcasting
Running	Back-stitching	Herringboning
Gathering	Slip-stitching	Buttonholing

Fancy Stitches

Fanning	Honeycombing	Cross-stitch
Feather-stitching	Smocking	French Knot

Tacking

Tacking is the stitch used when fixing two materials securely together (after they have been pinned), so that they may be correctly stitched. Cotton of a contrasting colour to the material which is to be tacked should be used, as it is more easily seen and removed when the stitching has been done.

The stitch is made by taking up a small piece of material on the needle, and passing over a larger piece—thus forming a long stitch on the uppermost side (see diagram 4).

Diagram 4—Tacking

This style of tacking is suitable for fixing the material of a skirt to its lining, etc., and must always be done flat on the table or skirt board. For fixing *seams*, either for trying on or for stitching, the tacking stitches must be of a more equal size (see diagram 5).

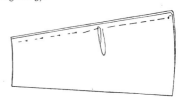

Diagram 5—Tacking for seams

In tacking the seams of a *bodice*, or wherever greater firmness is required, it is advisable to make an occasional "back-stitch," so that the tacking may be more secure for fitting. Otherwise the seams would "give" when being fitted, and would be too tight when the seams were *stitched*.

N.B.—The back-stitches must all be *cut* before the tacking is removed. For fixing *silk* or *velvet*, needles or steel pins should be used for *pinning* and fine silk for tacking, and *every* stitch should be cut before removal, to avoid marking the material.

Basting

Basting is another method of tacking, but is only suitable for tacking skirts to the lining, or for portions of the dress where large spaces have to be covered—not for seams. The stitch is worked as shown in diagram 6. It should always be done with the material lying flat on the table or board.

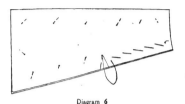

Diagram 6

Running

Running is a stitch made by taking up the same amount of material as is passed over ; all the stitches must be of equal length.

If the material is thin and soft, several stitches can be taken on to the needle before the thread is drawn through.

Gathering

Gathering is very much like running, except that only *half* the amount of material is taken up on the needle as that which is *passed over*, thus forming a short stitch on the wrong side, and one twice the length on the right.

If a second row of gathering is required below the first, the *stitches* must *exactly* correspond with the row above (see diagram 7), and the two threads must be drawn up simultaneously. If more than two rows of gathering are required, they must be done in the same way.

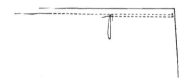

Diagram 7

Hemming

A hem is a double fold of material, and the stitch used to secure the fold is called hemming.

For materials such as linen, zephyr, muslin, cambric, etc., the raw edge can be turned down and firmly creased the whole length of the frill (or otherwise) which is to be hemmed, and if the hem is only to be a narrow one, a second turning the same width can be made, and firmly creased down.

N.B.—Narrow hems need not be tacked, but wide ones (in which the *first* turning should only just be wide enough to prevent the raw edges from fraying) ought always to be tacked securely first, also hems in woollen materials which will not crease.

The stitch is worked from right to left, the needle must be inserted in a slanting direction just below the edge of the hem, and pushed through just *above* it. These stitches must be taken all along the hem in a continuous line, a few threads apart, and they must all be made the same length (see diagram 8).

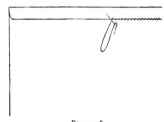

Diagram 8

Stitching

In stitching, as in hemming, only one stitch can be worked at a time. Take up a *small* piece of material on the needle, draw it through, and put the needle in *exactly* where the stitch was *commenced*, bringing it out in front of the stitch, leaving a space *exactly* the same length as the space covered by the stitch just made.

Work a continuous row of these stitches, *exactly meeting* one another and of the same length, to the end of the seam, or whatever is being stitched. The beauty of stitching depends on the uniform length of each stitch, and on the straightness of the stitched line.

Back-stitching

The only difference between this and stitching is, that instead of putting the needle back to *meet* the last stitch, it is carried only *half* way back, leaving a space between each stitch, thus forming a broken, instead of a continuous, line of stitching (see diagram 9).

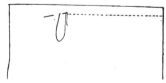

Diagram 9

Back stitching can be used instead of stitching in any part of the garment where less firmness and strength is required.

To be continued

Continued from page 73, Part 1.

SECOND LESSON. SEAMS

Lapped Seams—Strapped Seams—How to Make the Strapping—Cording and Piping

Seams

THERE are various methods of making seams in tailoring. In the one most frequently used the two pieces of material are placed together, the right side of the one piece facing the right side of the other, and machine stitched together on the wrong side.

The width of the turning left beyond the stitching depends on the make of the material —e.g., if a firm, closely woven cloth is being used, a narrow turning, about half an inch in width, is sufficient ; but if the material is of a loose make and likely to fray, such as serge, etc., the turning must be wider, or the seam will not wear. When stitched, the turnings of this seam are usually separated and pressed flat.

Lapped Seams

There are two methods of making lapped seams. One is to *stitch* the seams together as just described, but instead of *separating* the turnings, they should be turned over the same side, and pressed *double*. The pressing must *always* be done on the wrong side.

It is advisable to cut the one turning slightly narrower than the other, so as to graduate the thickness to avoid, as far as possible, marking the material on the right side by a thick edge of turnings.

A row of ornamental stitching can then be made on the *right* side of the garment, on and *close* to the edge of the seam, or about half an inch from it.

Another method is to turn in the raw edge of *one* piece of the material *on* the line which has been marked (for *stitching* the seam) by tailor tacking, and tack it down so that the row of tailor tacking is along the *edge*.

The piece of material to which it is to be joined should be placed flat on the table, right side uppermost, and the piece with the tacked down edge placed on it, also right side uppermost, covering the raw edge of the piece on the table, pinned and then tacked, so that the turned down edge just meets the tailor tacked line of the under piece.

A row of machine stitching must then be made on the right side on, and *close* to the edge of the seam. A second row can, if desired, be placed about a quarter of an inch or more from the first row.

In a skirt the lapped seam usually turns towards the back.

In a coat with lapped seams the centre *back* seam must be stitched slightly to one side, so that when the seam is lapped the *centre* of the back of the coat is *exactly* between the two rows of stitching, otherwise the back of the coat will be crooked.

The centre back seam is not always lapped, even though other seams may be so made. In that case, the back seam would, of course, be stitched down the *centre*.

The shoulder seams usually lap over towards the back.

Sometimes the *back* seam of a sleeve is lapped (towards the back), but the *inside* seam is never lapped.

Strapped Seams

Strapping is used on the seams of coats and skirts ; it is also used as a trimming, put on in rows and in patterns.

The material to be used for the strapping should be cut just double the width the strapping is to be when finished, and *exactly* on the bias. The simplest way to do this is to place the material on the table, face downwards, measure the number of inches of the *width* of the material, measure the same number on the selvedge, and make a chalk mark.

Take a tailor's square or a long rule and draw a straight line from the chalk mark to the opposite corner (see diagram 9). This line will be exactly on the bias, or cross, of the material.

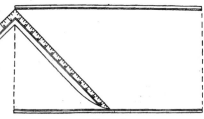

Diagram 9
How to find the bias of a material

N.B.—Crêpe, serge, or any diagonal material should be cut *across* the diagonal, and not with it (diagram 10).

From the line just drawn measure double the width the strapping is to be when

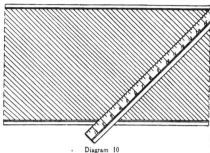

Diagram 10
How to cut diagonal material on the cross

finished. Place chalk marks at short intervals, and with the square or rule draw a straight line through these chalk marks from one selvedge to the other. Continue to measure in this way until a sufficient number of strips have been marked to make the quantity of strapping required. Carefully cut through the chalk lines, join all the strips together evenly to form one long straight strip, with the edges all *perfectly* level. Note that the thread of the material of all the strips must run the same (the selvedge) way. In the short strips that are cut from the corner, and not from selvedge to selvedge, it is necessary to cut off a piece from the cut edge of each piece (before it is pinned to another strip) to make the thread run in the same direction (diagram 11). It is better to join the shorter strips to the longer ones, instead of putting all the short ones together, as the joins are not so observable.

To Make the Strapping

When the strips have been stitched together, separate the turnings and press them flat, turn down (on the wrong side) the raw edge of one side to the middle of the strip of material, and tack it. Turn down the other edge to meet the first, and tack this also.

To ensure the strapping being perfectly straight, this tacking must be very neatly and evenly done.

The strapping must now be pressed on the wrong side *very carefully*, so as not to stretch it. It is now ready to be tacked on to the garment for stitching.

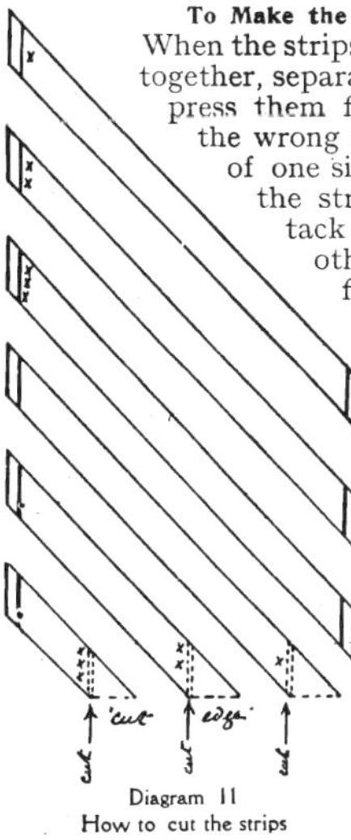

Diagram 11
How to cut the strips

D 18

Very good tailors generally prepare the strapping by placing the two raw edges together, and *sewing them over* before tacking it flat, especially when the strapping is to be used for the seams of coats.

The stitching on of the strapping must be done as near to the edge as possible.

For drill or other washing coats which are to be made unlined, the seams of the coat can be made on the right side, the turnings cut level, separated, pressed flat, and then covered over and made neat with the strapping.

Cording and Piping

To prepare the material for cording, cut strips from ¾ to 1 inch in width (according to the thickness of the cord which is to be placed in them), and *perfectly* on the cross. Join the strips together and press open the seams on the wrong side.

If it is required to join one piece of the garment to another by cording (such as the seams of a skirt or the flounce on to a skirt), place a cord along the *centre* of the strip, turn the material over it, push the cord well up into the fold, and run (through the *double* material) *close* under the cord.

The material for the piping for cording the top of a skirt, or the *edge* of any part of the garment, is cut, joined, and pressed in the same way, but, instead of the cord being placed along the *centre* of the strip, it is placed about one-third from the edge; the material is then turned over it, and the cord well pushed up into the fold. It is then run through the *double* material, as *close as possible* under the cord.

Cording and piping are usually made and put on by hand, as the ordinary presser foot of the sewing machine does not allow of the stitching being made *close* enough to the cord. A special presser foot, however, can be purchased with which cording can be made and put on; the price is about 3s. 6d. If much cording has to be done, it is well worth this small outlay, as, besides being much quicker than hand work, it is much firmer and also looks better.

An ornamental cord can be sewn as a trimming to the edge of any garment, such as revers and collar of a coat, etc. This cord can, of course, be bought ready made, or plaited by the home-worker.

It is put on in the following way: Place the cord along the edge and on the *right* side of the garment (the cord held next the worker) and over-sew it on; roll back the cord and press the stitches well down with the thumb-nail, so that the cord may lie flat along the outer edge of the revers or other part of the garment. Another variety of cord for ornamental trimming can be made and sewn on in a pattern (as braid would be) to a dress or coat. This cord is made from *piece* silk or satin cut *perfectly* on the cross into strips about one inch wide. These strips must be joined together into one length, and the seams pressed on the wrong side.

Q

21

Three or four strands (according to the thickness of the cord required) of fingering wool are then placed in the centre of the strip (instead of a cotton cord), and one raw edge of the silk or satin is rolled over the wool as tightly as possible, the other raw edge is then turned in and hemmed down over it.

To be continued.

DRESS FOR BUSINESS WEAR

In Your Dress be Simple—And Practical—Coat and Skirt—Blouses—Office Sleeves

THE woman or girl in business is always confronted with the problem of how to dress suitably, and at the same time to retain her feminine personality; also, the necessity for strict economy governs and limits her choice. The secret of good dressing at any time is that the dress should be appropriate to the occasion.

The girl who travels to her office every day is confronted with many vicissitudes of wind and weather, and she must content herself with severely practical clothing. Suitability must be the keynote of her scheme, and so attired she will never be out of place.

From the employer's point of view, the appearance of his office may be considerably lowered by the unsuitable attire of his women staff. Appropriate dressing, therefore, is appreciated, although no word may be passed on the subject.

An abundance of jewellery is out of place. Many rings, long chains, or clinking bangles are a distraction both to the wearer and her fellow-workers.

Her hair should be arranged neatly, and she should avoid any style of hairdressing that requires constant readjustment during the day, as this wastes her employer's time.

The chief items for everyday wear in the business woman's outfit are : Coat and skirt, blouses, shoes, gloves, hats, a showerproof or rubber coat, and a long, warm coat for cold weather. With these, she will find herself provided with the essentials.

Coat and Skirt

This costume is the most useful, and it allows variety to be obtained by a change of blouse and neck fitments. It should be well cut and tailored. Decorations may consist either of stitchings or flat braids, since fancy trimmings hold the dust and need constant renewal.

Many tailors make a speciality of trimly-built costumes, made to measure, from two guineas ; also, by watching the best shops excellent models may be secured, ready made, at quite reasonable prices. On no account should money be invested in a cheap material ; it is far better to obtain a good costume once in two years than a cheap one each season.

The skirt should clear the ground all round, and be finished with an efficient inside hem of material or lining. The addition of some kind of skirt protector to prevent the edge cutting through is also essential. This may consist of a "brush-edge," sold by the yard, in every shade, by all drapers, or crossway strips of velveteen ; but whichever is used its value as a skirt protector depends on its being sewn securely

to project slightly beyond the skirt. These points are worth attention, or constant renewal will be necessary.

For summer, light-weight all-wool tweeds, serges, or alpacas are suitable fabrics, and will be found more satisfactory than plain-faced cloths, which soil very readily, and often spot badly in the rain.

Both coat and skirt may be as smart as desired in cut, but passing novelties in design should be avoided, since a pronounced change in fashion would date them too accurately.

If the dress allowance permits, some linen or cotton frocks will be both cool and healthy in hot weather, but by most women the laundry bill also must be considered.

For winter wear a warmer tweed or serge, with a lined skirt, will be required. Navy blue serge is quite an ideal material, and, if possible, should form a reserve costume.

In economical dressing it is a distinct saving to have two costumes in wear at the same time. All garments wear better if given a "rest," and, with a little management, this can be arranged, even on a limited allowance.

Another practical style is the "Princess," with removable vest and under-sleeves. These, if made of all-over lace, net, or even silk, can easily be washed at home ; and such a gown, worn with a coat to match, will prove a welcome change from the blouse and short skirt.

Blouses

Here the personal taste of the wearer may be permitted to hold sway to some extent. Pretty delaines, cambrics, simply trimmed with embroidery, or the more severe "shirt," may be equally worn. Cheap lace trimmings, transparent low yokes and elbow sleeves are not in good taste for office wear.

Office work is detrimental to the sleeves of a blouse or dress. The paper cuff pinned on is not altogether satisfactory, as it is apt to cut the wrist. Half-sleeves of cambric, such as nurses wear, are eminently practical, and can be easily washed as required, or removable cuffs or half-sleeves made of all-over embroidered muslin, answer the purpose equally well, and are decidedly smarter. Cut quite plainly, a single button will secure it at the wrist, or the seam may be joined its entire length, to slip over the hand. A single pin will fasten the half-sleeve in position, or an elastic, a little smaller than the top of the sleeve, may be sewn in to just fit the arm closely.

To be continued.

The following are good firms for supplying materials, etc., mentioned in this Section : Messrs. Horrockses' Longcloths and Sheetings (Wholesale only) ; London Glove Co. (Gloves) ; Lutas Leathley & Co. (Dress Fabrics).

WOMAN'S DRESS

Conducted by the Editress of "Fashions for All"

In this important section of EVERY WOMAN'S ENCYCLOPÆDIA every aspect of dress will be dealt with by practical and experienced writers. The history of dress from earliest times will be told, and practical and useful information will be given in:

Home Dressmaking		Millinery
How to Cut Patterns	*Home Tailoring*	*Lessons in Hat Trimming*
Methods of Self-measure-	*Representative Fashions*	*How to Make a Shape*
ment	*Fancy Dress*	*How to Curl Feathers*
Colour Contrasts	*Alteration of Clothes, etc.*	*Flowers, Hat-pins, Colours, etc.*
Boots and Shoes	**Furs**	**Gloves**
Choice	*Choice*	*Choice*
How to Keep in Good Condition	*How to Preserve, etc.*	*Cleaning, etc.*
How to Soften Leather, etc.	*How to Detect Frauds*	**Jewellery, etc.**

PRACTICAL MILLINERY

By MRS. ERIC PRITCHARD

Continued from page 229, Part 2

The Art of Choosing Fabrics—How to Make Bows—The Charms of Colour Schemes—Individuality of Taste

IN my last article I left the "shape" completed in cloth, satin, or velvet ready for whatever trimming might be selected. Trimmings, of course, alter with different seasons of the year, and follow wild flights of fashion. We must remember that we Englishwomen have a somewhat deserved reputation for using decoration on hats with a distinctly heavy and all too lavish hand. I will commence by describing one of the most popular forms of trimming—namely, the bow. There are, at the moment of writing, many pretty and large hats trimmed with wide bows of velvet or satin, and lined with a contrasting colour, just as there are small toques adorned with "choux," and wonderfully constructed rosettes. But bows and bow-making are quite an independent part of millinery. We must first of all *choose our fabrics* with care both in respect to quantity as well as to quality.

One of the newest ideas is to line the loops of our bows with a material known as *tapestry galon*—a lovely model seen in Paris had a bow made of a piece of velvet edged with a piping cord and partly lined or edged with a narrow galon of tapestry. Since this idea is fairly simple of construction and most effective, I am adopting the idea for our bow.

Purchase ⅝ yard black velvet, about 21 inches wide, the usual price at West End drapers' for a good millinery velvet being 4s. 11½d. per yard. (Be careful not to get too *blue a black*; the *cheaper* velvets err in this direction.) Buy a skein of narrow black piping cord, at 1½d. The tapestry galon should be 2 inches wide, and is obtainable at 1s. 0¾d. per yard—3¾ yards will be required.

Fig. 1

Fold the velvet into three longitudinal layers, cut, and leave three lengths measuring ⅝ yard by 7 inches wide, as illustrated.

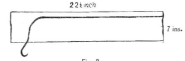

Fig. 2

Take one length, and place the piping cord on the *wrong* side, ½ inch from the edge. See Fig. 2.

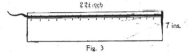

Fig. 3

Turn material or velvet over, pin cord in.

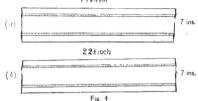

(*a*)

(*b*)

Fig. 4

Sew cord *neatly* in, as illustrated, and repeat the same process on the other edge of fabric, and also on all other lengths, the 22½ inch by 7 inch pieces being destined for loops of bow.

11¼ inch

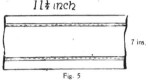

7 ins.

Fig. 5

Cut your third length into two equal halves, thus making two lengths measuring 11¼ inches by 7 inches, the one piece being for the extra short loop, the other for the tie-over one ; repeat directions for Figs. 2, 3, 4.

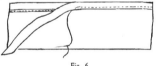

Fig. 6

Take one length of the velvet, place galon ¼ inch from edge on wrong side, and sew on to the piping cord (being careful not to take stitches through), repeat the same on the other side, and on remaining four lengths.

The separate pieces (Figs. 4 and 5) being now completed, we proceed to *shape* our bow.

Fig. 7

Double over the two longest lengths (*right side* being *outside*), and sew as illustrated.

Fig. 8

Join the two longest loops together.

Fig. 9

Sew the bow (the two long loops that have been thus joined) to the centre front of the crown of the hat, taking stitches through crown to ensure firmness.

Fig. 10

Make one of the remaining small pieces of velvet into a loop, and sew on to right side of crown.

Fig. 11

The tie-over plays an important part in the success of the bow. To attain this tie-over, take the *last* short length and sew on to brim of hat about 1½ inches from the crown (not allowing stitches to show through the brim).

Fig. 12

Throw the tie-over in an artistic manner to meet the loop on the *right* side.

Fig. 13

Catch end of this tie-over very neatly at the back of the loop and sew firmly.

I must impress on my readers that although great neatness and exactitude must be observed in the measurements and finishing off of all trimmings, they must not be too much *sewn* on to the hat itself.

24

How often we hear the remark: "You can tell that is a *French* hat by the lightness of the bow," and it is an undeniable fact that it is very difficult to acquire this light touch. Great care should be taken in handling such fabrics as velvet and silk, as if the bloom gets rubbed off, the trimming looks "messy" and unsmart. Some people are born with the artistic tendency, but an artistic training is also essential in all matters relating to millinery; and the well-known successful millinery houses of Paris and London always possess some man or woman designer, who has what can only be described

Shows the model completely finished, the loops of the bow being lined with delightful contrasts in colour

as individuality of taste. It is this individuality that produces those wonderful specimens of headgear that, used, as models, procure for their firm such startling prices—£10 to £20 for a Paris model is by no means an uncommon sum to be given by English and American buyers in well-known Parisian houses.

It is, therefore, an error to suppose that any amount of feathers or beautiful materials can make a smart and marketable hat—the essence of success lies in the magic word "style," still better expressed by the French as "chic," and this is only attained by hard study and much practice.

PRACTICAL LESSONS IN DRESSMAKING

Continued from page 231, Part 2

By M. PRINCE BROWNE

Examiner in Dressmaking, Tailoring, French Pattern Modelling, Plain Needlework, and Millinery, of the Teachers in Training at the University College of South Wales and Monmouthshire, Cardiff; the London Higher Technical Examination Centres, etc.; First Class Diploma for Tailoring; Diploma of Honour for Dressmaking; Diploma of Merit of the Highest Order for Teaching; Silver Medallist, London Exhibition, 1900; Silver Medal, Franco-British Exhibition, 1908; Author of "Up-to-Date Dresscutting and Drafting," also "The Practical Work of Dressmaking and Tailoring."

THIRD LESSON

Slip-stitching—Sewing—Overcasting—Herringboning—Button-holing and Button-holes—
"Fanning"—Feather-stitching

Slip-stitching

SLIP-STITCHING is used to invisibly fasten down hems, facings, etc., and to fix false tucks (cut on the cross) on to skirts, etc.

If a hem is to be slip-stitched, turn down a double fold, as for an ordinary hem, and tack it. Thread a needle with fine silk to match the material, take up a mere thread of it *under* the fold with the needle, and draw it gently through.

Slip the needle *into* and *along* the *inside* of the fold, and make a short running stitch; draw the needle through and again take up a thread of the material *under* the fold, and so continue to the end.

Slip-stitching is worked from right to left.

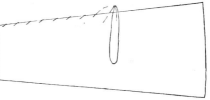

Diagram 9

Overcasting

Overcasting is a stitch used to protect the raw edges of seams to prevent their fraying; it somewhat resembles sewing, but is worked from *left* to *right*, instead of from *right* to *left*, and the stitches are made larger and further apart. They should form a row of slanting stitches all of equal size and depth, as shown in diagram 9.

Herringboning

Herringbone-stitch is used in dressmaking to fasten down the raw edges, when a false hem or a facing is to be put on, to keep the turnings in position and make them lie flat. It can also be used on thick materials instead of hemming, to avoid the double fold of material. The stitch is worked from *left* to *right*, and forms two rows of stitches, the threads crossing each other diagonally.

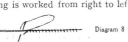

Diagram 8

Sewing

Sewing is a stitch used more frequently in plain needlework than in dressmaking; it is, however, useful for joining two pieces of material together, after the raw edges have been turned in, such as the ends of neck, waist, and wrist-bands. Also for sewing cord to the edge of a garment. This stitch is worked from right to left, as shown in diagram 8.

To make the stitch, insert the needle from right to left, first above and then

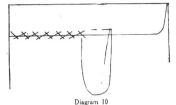

Diagram 10

below the raw edge ; the *lower* side of each stitch should come just under the raw edge of the fold, the *upper* side of the stitch *on* the fold, but *not* through to the right side of the dress. When the stitch is finished it should appear as in diagram 10.

Button-holing and Button-holes

In dressmaking, button-holes are worked from left to right. Pass the needle through the slit, and take up the amount of material required for the depth of the stitch. While the needle is in this position, carry the twist from the eye over to the left of the needle and *under* the point to the *right*, draw the needle out rather sharply towards the slit, so as to form a little knot or purl edge, round the opening. When the garment is ready for the button-holes, take a piece of card and measure the diameter of the button to be used, and notch the card to that width. Mark the position and length for the button-holes before cutting them (a long stitch in cotton of a contrasting colour can be placed where each button-hole is to be cut). Punch a small hole on the *outside* ends of each mark, then, with a small, sharp pair of scissors, cut a slit for the button-hole to the length marked by the notch on the card.

N.B.—It is very important that the slit should be cut *perfectly straight*, as a good button-hole can never be made if the edges are crooked and uneven. The punched hole and the slit should now appear as in diagram 11, but, as the button-hole should be pear-shaped, a small piece must be cut off on each side,

Diagrams 11, 12, and 13

from the slit into the round hole, to give it the shape shown in diagram 12. Great care must be taken to cut the two sides *exactly* alike, or the button-hole will have a crooked appearance. If the material in which the button-holes are to be worked is likely to fray, it is better to oversew round each one first with fine silk of the same colour. It is unnecessary to oversew the cut edge of any firmly woven material, muslin, or print.

The button-holes must be worked with twist to match the material, and the work commenced from the side of the straight slit (not the pear-shaped end). In working

the button-hole care must be taken to catch the under layer, or layers, of material in with the button-hole stitches, or they will slip away and remain unworked. When the button-hole has been worked all round it must be "barred" ; this is done by working two or three straight stitches *across* the end of the button-hole and two or three threads beyond the beginning of the slit, drawing the two edges of the work close together, but not allowing them to overlap. Button-hole *over* these straight stitches, bring the purl of each stitch towards the slit, and take the first and last stitch through the *material*, so as to give firmness to the bar, and keep it in position.

The button-holes are sometimes worked (before the slit is cut) along each side of the *mark* for the button-hole with a row of running stitches, fastened off firmly ; this prevents the button-hole stretching when it is worked.

If a punch is not available, the hole can be cut with a small, sharp pair of scissors by snipping the ends of the slit in a slanting direction, as shown in diagram 13, and then cutting *out* a small curved piece, as denoted by the *dotted* line in the same diagram, but as it is impossible to cut these ends with the scissors exactly to match in a row of button-holes, it is well worth the small outlay for the punch.

N.B.—The "punch" is described and illustrated in the First Lesson on Tailoring.

FANCY STITCHES
"Fanning"

Fanning is an ornamental stitch used for fixing the top of bones. After a bodice has been boned, a "fan" of stitches is worked near the top of each one ; it consists of a long centre stitch, on *each* side of which two or three stitches of graduated length are worked, each of the five (or seven, as the case may be) stitches must diverge from the same hole at the bottom.

Thread a long, *strong* needle with twist, and pass it from the *under* side of the bone (about one inch below the top end) and *right through* the centre of it ; pass the needle back to the under-side, about a quarter of an inch from the top, and *exactly* through the *centre* of the bone.

This will form the long centre stitch. Bring the needle up again through the same hole as at first, and make a shorter stitch on one side, and slightly apart from it ; make one or more stitches on the same side, each one rather shorter than the last, and the same distance apart ; work stitches to correspond on the other side of the centre stitch. Pass the needle (eye foremost) twice or three times under and over these five (or seven, as the case may be) stitches. This will form a stem, and hold them in position (diagram 14). Pass the needle through to the under side of the bone, fasten off the twist securely, and cut it off.

Diagram 14

26

N.B.—The colour of the twist is a matter of taste, but it should always be of the same shade as that used for the cross-stitch fixing the " tight band " to the bodice and marking the centre of the skirt.

Feather-stitching

Feather-stitching is occasionally used to ornament garments in place of ordinary stitching; it is effective and can be easily learned. In dressmaking it is most suitable for blouses, cotton or linen dresses, and children's garments. It can be worked in embroidery or crochet cotton, silk, or wool, according to the material on which it is to be done.

As a guide to ensure the straightness of the work, a line of tacking may be made along the band, or otherwise, where the feather-stitching is to be, and the stitches are then worked alternately *right* and *left* of the line of tacking, and the cotton, silk, or wool must always be carried under the point of the needle (at each stitch) so as to form a loop. The needle should be slightly slanted towards the line of tacking in working each stitch, as this gives the work a less stiff appearance than if the needle is inserted perfectly *straight*.

Diagram 15

The size of the stitches depends on the material, but they must be of uniform length, and the tendency to *increase* the size of the stitch as the work proceeds must be guarded against. The finer the material the smaller the stitch should be.

Feather-stitching may be single, double, or treble—either *one* stitch alternately right and left of the line of tacking, or *two* stitches alternately right and left, or *three* to the right and three to the left. Diagram 15 illustrates the work.

N.B.—The cotton, wool, or silk, must never be drawn too tightly or the appearance of the feather-stitching will be spoilt.

To be continued.

PRACTICAL LESSONS IN TAILORING
FOR HOME WORKERS AND OTHERS
By M. PRINCE BROWNE

Examiner in Dressmaking, Tailoring, French Pattern Modelling, Millinery, and Plain Needlework, of the Teachers in Training at the University College of South Wales and Monmouthshire, Cardiff, the London Technical Examination Centre, etc. Author of " Up-to-Date Dresscutting and Drafting," also " The Practical Work of Dressmaking and Tailoring."

Continued from page 231, Part 2

THIRD LESSON. POCKETS
Cording—Coat Pockets—How to Make a Flap Pocket

THE ornamental cord, made from silk or satin, described in the last lesson, is now ready to be put on. The design having been previously traced on the material of which the garment is to be made, the cord must be carefully tacked on to it (right through the cord), with a fine needle threaded with silk (preferably), or with fine, soft cotton. The cord must not be twisted, or the appearance will be quite spoiled ; nor must it be strained in turning round the curves of the design, or the material will be drawn up and puckered. The lines of the tracing of the design must be completely covered. When the tacking on is completed, the cord can be sewn on either from the wrong side of the material by a fine running stitch, and an occasional back stitch, or finely slip-stitched on with strong silk, on the right side. The stitches must be taken *well under* the cord, as they must not be seen, and they must not be drawn too tightly.

N.B.—The method of slip-stitching is described in the lesson on dressmaking.

In selecting a design for this style of trimming, a running pattern, the lines of which *do not cross*, should be chosen.

In removing the tacking threads, *each stitch* should be cut before drawing them out. If the work requires pressing when finished, the *wrong* side of it must be passed over an inverted iron—it must not be pressed flat on a table or board.

Coat Pockets

The materials required for making the pockets for coats are a piece of the cloth and a piece of the lining which are to be used for making the coat, French canvas, linen (black or white), tacking cotton, machine silk. The French canvas ought always to be shrunk before it is used, and to ensure this, it is advisable for the worker to do it herself.

To shrink the canvas, open it out and place it flat on the bare ironing-board or table ; take a piece of linen (an old piece will do), put it into a basin of water, and then wring it out as dry as possible. Open it out and place it over the canvas, and with a warm iron or tailor's goose press well all over the damp cloth; remove the cloth and continue pressing the canvas until it is quite dry, and has regained its ordinary firmness. Cloth can be shrunk in the same way, placed *wrong* side uppermost on the board; but as cloth should be shrunk while it is still in the piece, and as it is rather heavy work, as well as a difficult thing for an amateur, it is well worth the extra sixpence per yard which is the charge usually made for having it done at the shop where the cloth has been purchased. If the cloth is to be shrunk before making, it is advisable to purchase about half a yard more than is necessary for a costume.

To Make a Flap Pocket

The size of the flap for the pocket is decided by the length and style the coat is to be made. The flap should be interlined with French canvas, which must be cut on the straight (which prevents its stretching), and with a *perfectly straight edge all round*. It may be cut about 4½ or 5 inches in length, and 2¼ or 2½ inches in depth, according to the size required. No extra is required for turnings. This gives the net size of the flap, and allows a quarter of an inch on the upper edge for stitching it into the coat.

The cloth must now be cut.

Place the piece of canvas for the flap along, and quite level with, the cut edge of the cloth, and cut it out, allowing good turnings on the two ends, and a small turning on the lower edge; the extra large turning on the two ends is to allow of the cloth being " eased " when it is tacked over the canvas. If this is not done the corners of the flap will turn up.

N.B.—If the cloth is one with a " face," care must be taken to make the flap so that the " face " will smooth downwards.

When the worker has learnt how to make the various pockets and is sufficiently advanced to make a coat—the coat must be cut out first—and when the position for the pockets has been decided upon, the cloth for the flaps must be cut at the correct angle to match the grain in the cloth of the fronts—*e.g.*, if the flap is to be parallel with the waist-line, the cloth can be cut quite straight across the cut edge of the material; but if the flap is to slope downwards the cloth must be sloped at the top and at the bottom, so that it may match the grain on the front of the coat, and any check or stripe in the cloth must also be matched on the flap.

Tack the cloth on to the canvas, with the cloth uppermost, and with the work held over the hand, so that the cloth may be " eased " in tacking it on to the canvas. Still holding the cloth uppermost, turn it over the edge of the canvas, and tack it neatly down, near the edge of the two ends and along the bottom, but do not turn the cloth over the top edge. In turning the corners, cut away all the superfluous material, and make them as flat as possible, but be careful not to make the cuts too deep, or the raw edges of the cloth will show.

Before the flap is stitched all round, it must be well pressed on the wrong side, under a damp cloth.

N.B.—It is always well to press any work which is to be stitched round the edge before the stitching is done, as it makes the edge flat and sharp, and enables the worker to do the stitching nearer the edge and more evenly.

Machine stitch one or more rows, according to the number intended to be placed on the rest of the coat, round the sides and bottom edge of the flap. It must now be lined with a piece of lining to match that of the coat. The lining should first be tacked on (not " eased," or the corners will turn up), then turned in near the edge to cover the stitching on the wrong side, tacked again, and neatly felled with silk to match the lining. Again press the flap on the wrong side with a dry cloth over it.

It is now ready to be put into the coat, but as this is a lesson on pockets only, and the worker has not yet learnt to make a coat, the flap can be put into a piece of cloth, and the pocket made in that, instead of in the front of a coat.

With a rule or tailor's square draw a chalk line on the right side of the piece of cloth for the position of the pocket, and on it mark the exact length of the flap.

Cut on the straight (along the selvedge) a strip of linen, about two inches longer than the flap and about two inches in width; place this on to the wrong side of the cloth, exactly under the chalk line (leaving an equal length of linen beyond the line at each end), and tack it on from the right side by a line of tacking along the chalk line.

Take the flap and place it, wrong side uppermost, on the right side of the piece of cloth, with the raw edge on the chalk line and the finished edge turned upwards toward the top of the piece of cloth; or, if on a coat, towards the neck of it. Tack it firmly in this position along, but not too near, the raw edge; cut two pieces of lining (to match the lining in the flap) rather longer than the flap and the depth the pockets are desired to be made. Place one of these pieces, wrong side uppermost, over the flap, with the cut edge level with the raw edge of the flap, leaving the same amount of lining beyond the flap on each side.

Place the second piece of lining, wrong side uppermost, in the opposite direction, the raw edges of both pieces meeting on the chalk line, and tack them both to the cloth in this position. Machine stitch both pieces of lining on to the cloth along the raw edges, and as near to the chalk line as the material and lining will allow without fraying.

The lines of stitching must be perfectly even and parallel, and *exactly* the same length; they must only extend the length of the flap, and must not be continued across the corners, or they will not set flat when the opening is cut, and the lining is turned inside.

To be continued.

PRACTICAL ADVICE ON THE CHOICE OF FURS

By THE HON. MRS. FITZROY STEWART

No. 3.—SEALSKINS

Durability—Alaska Seals—Characteristics of Seals—How they are Killed—The Sealskin Coat—
The Musquash

SEALSKIN, in the opinion of many, exceeds all other fur in beauty and value. It certainly has some signal advantages. Sealskin is noted for its durability. In this respect it comes after sea-otter—the most durable of all furs—and far ahead of sable, ermine, silver fox, blue fox, and the fatally delicate chinchilla. Then, to the touch, it is softer and more silky than the finest silk, and to say that it feels "like sealskin" is the only description of its exquisite texture. Also, it adapts itself better than any other fur to garments which are cut to fit the figure closely ; and, best of all praise, its dark, rich tone makes it most becoming to a woman with a good complexion. In fact, fine sealskin is now as much sought after as Russian sable.

On the other hand, sealskin is a heavier fur than either sable, ermine, broadtail, or chinchilla, and is also more weighty than its poorer relation, musquash. But sealskins, as now cured, are half as light again as they were a decade or so ago ; and the younger the animal the lighter its skin, as may be easily imagined. As a result, the young seals are far more valuable than their older companions.

The cost of Alaska seal will soon become prohibitive. The chief supply comes from the Behring Sea, and the take is now regulated by the treaty of 1894 between Great Britain and the United States of America. At the time of writing, a long coat of the best Alaska would cost from £180 to £200 ; and the value of this fur will increase, as the price of good skins is, rising in a reckless manner. Next in quality comes what is known as North-West sealskin, and a coat made of the finest skins could be procured for about £150.

Alaska seals comprise the male seals taken by the American Commercial Company in the Pribylov Islands, in the Behring Sea. These skins are the best because they come from an Arctic climate. The seals found further south have much poorer skins, for careful Nature provides the creatures who live far North with a thicker coat than those who dwell in warmer and more southern regions.

As regards seal fur, an expert states a curious fact, namely, that the number of hairs on a baby skin is as great as those on a full-grown and, of course, much larger animal. Hence the fur is closer on the younger ones, by which token a young Alaska seal is the most precious of the entire species.

The North - West seals are those taken by the pelagic (deep-sea) sealers off the western coasts of North America.

The seal is an amphibious creature, can swim and dive, and its movements in the water are extremely graceful. On land it moves in rather a clumsy fashion.

The male seal, when full-grown, measures six feet or more in length, and weighs at least four hundred pounds. Its head is small, its eyes large and expressive, and the upper lip bears a long, stiff moustache. The fore feet, or "flippers," are a pair of dark bluish-black hands, with no suggestion of fingers, but the hind feet, which are longer, have loose, slender, ribbon-like toes, that were described by an American traveller as being "like a pair of black kid gloves flattened out and shrivelled." The female is smaller in size, but her head and large black eyes are strikingly beautiful.

Seals have their peculiarities. One of these is that the outer ear is almost

A Sealskin Coat such as this is a precious possession. Before one is bought it should be very carefully examined, since sealskin is imitated more easily than sable

Photo : Reutlinger

entirely wanting ; and another, that they have the strange habit of swallowing large stones, for which no reason has as yet been discovered.

They take kindly to the water, and a seal has been known to stay under for quite twenty minutes. But seals possess all the five senses to great perfection. Their hearing seems to be acute, and they are much affected by the sound of music. A flute is said to attract them to a boat, when they have not learned caution by experience.

The ringing of church bells at Hoy, in Orkney, often causes their appearance in the little bay, which is almost landlocked. In a word, travellers who have spent much time in observing the ways and manners of these creatures, declare that they exhibit a high order of instinct, even of intelligence.

The season for seals begins in March, and lasts for about three months. The vessels engaged in this trade belong, in most cases, to Newfoundland. The crews land on the ice, and drive the herds to the " killing grounds," which are situated close to the villages. Here they are allowed to rest until they become cool. If killed while heated, the hair comes off in the skinning process, and the pelt is thereby ruined.

The seals are killed by club, knife, or rifle. The pelagic sealers, of course, have a different method. These hunters go from their ships in boats, paddle up to the seals, and spear them as they sleep on the surface of the water.

The fur of the seal is found to be finest and thickest in its third or fourth year, and in their work the hunters employ great skill and discrimination.

With regard to the fur, anyone who has seen the seals at the Zoological Gardens will have noticed that their coat is long and hairy, not short and close as in sealskin. In real fact, the seal has two coats, one long and one short, and it is the under coat that furnishes the fine, silky pile which is seen in our sealskins.

One word as to the killing. It has often been said that these animals are killed in a cruel fashion. But, in a Government report, Professor Thompson testified as follows :

He said, " I could not detect in the whole process any cruelty, either intentional or accidental. With respect to the driving and killing, I, at least, have no recommendation to suggest for their improvement."

By the way, it is amusing to note that in the seal trade there is much eccentricity in nomenclature. It seems strange, for example, that a " bull " and a " cow " should occupy a " harem " on a " rookery," and bear a " pup," which, if a male, is a " bachelor " for

The male seal when full-grown measures six feet or more in length, and weighs at least four hundred pounds. The female is smaller in size

Photo : Berridge

the first four years of his life ; and also that the business of killing and skinning these animals should be known as a " fishery."

The curing of sealskin has risen to a fine art, and the best curing is now done in London. The American dressers have used every effort to handle sealskin with success, and have had to assist them a protective tariff. Yet, with every possible handicap, the London trade still excels in this branch of industry. Experts believe that the quality of our air and water may give an advantage to English dressers. In fact, the United Kingdom scores in several directions. Those who know declare that the excellence of Guinness's stout is due to the curious nature of the waters of the River Liffey ; and the superfine texture of the paper of which our Bank of England notes are made is said to owe its origin to the water of the River Test, near the Laverstoke mills, in Hampshire.

The process of dressing sealskin takes from one to three months, and the dyeing process is almost as intricate as the dressing. This latter seems to be the secret of success with our English seal furriers. They alone are able to dye the skins the deep, dark, rich brown which is now reckoned as a necessity.

At the same time, no injury must be done to the skins, and the dye must be thoroughly fixed, and to accomplish all this means skilful work, great patience, and much scientific experience. Every hair of a seal is, in reality, a tube which contains a minute quantity of oil, and for this reason the utmost care must be taken in preparing the skins, also the garments made from them should be treated with many precautions. For instance, sealskin should never be exposed to too great heat, such as drying before a fire, or the use of a hot iron, as the lustre of the fine fur would be thereby damaged. And if sealskin has been rained upon, it should be shaken and lightly beaten with a small cane, or, if much mischief has been done, it should be sent to a first-rate furrier.

The actual process of dyeing sealskin is as follows : The skins are first limed, and then packed back to back, with a layer of brown paper over the fur holes, in order to prevent the dye from penetrating the pelt, and thus damaging the skin. A coat of dye is then applied cold, and trodden in, after which the skins are dyed gradually. They have from nine to fourteen coats of colour brushed in, each coat drying before the next is applied.

By a new process, a darker top is acquired by dipping the skin in the liquid, which in this case must be warm, and, as a result, not so many coats of colour are required.

Next comes the important matter of the

making up of the skins into garments. This needs infinite care, because the skins must be matched in the most accurate manner.

The hair of sealskin varies in length not only in each skin, but in different parts of the same skin, and if there is but a fraction of an inch of difference in the length of the hairs, a ridge is at once made which detracts much from the beauty of the garment. In a well-made coat, no seam must be perceptible. In fact, much skilled labour is required, and when to this is added the price of the skins, no one need wonder that the cost of sealskin soars steadily upwards.

A sealskin coat is a precious possession, and a woman who buys such an expensive article should inspect the skins, and make her own selection. Fine, close pile, and soft, pliable felt are of first importance ; and it is also needful that all the skins should be uniform in size, colour, and quality. Sealskin is more easily imitated than sable, and a buyer should be well on her guard against dishonest practices. An expert has kindly given some useful information. He says that sealskin is less flat and much thicker and closer than either musquash or the so-called coney seal and electric seal. Here is one absolutely certain method of detecting frauds in sealskin :

The leather of sealskin is never dyed at all, only the fur, while musquash and its cheaper fellows are wholly dyed—the leather as well as the fur. Now, a would-be purchaser who has doubts should, if buying a made-up garment, undo a bit of the lining, by which means the fact of fraud can at once be ascertained.

All of us, however, cannot afford the cost of fine sealskin, and a useful substitute can now be procured. Musquash is a real skin, and by the removal of long hairs and other treatment, may be made to resemble seal so closely that a skilled furrier would at a short distance be unable to detect the difference. But there are not many shops where the "seal-finished," or "plucked," musquash can be found in such perfection that there is not a bluish sheen, instead of the true brown tint, in the undergrowth. Besides this, the leather is stiff and the edges weaker and poorer than those of sealskin ; and musquash is a very small skin as compared with seal—12 or 14 inches in length, as against 38 to 40 or 50 inches—and in looking even at the surface of a musquash coat, it is possible to perceive seams 8 or 10 inches apart, which, in a way, spoil its appearance. Musquash, however, is cheap as compared with sealskin. A coat of the best fur would cost from £40 to £60, and it would look well, and wear fairly well, and must be reckoned as a sound investment.

The musquash is a sort of rat, a native of North America. In shape it resembles the common rat, and its body is covered with a short, downy, dark-brown fur, intermixed with lighter and coarser hairs. It feeds chiefly on vegetables, and is an aquatic creature that seldom goes far from lakes and rivers.

Coney seal and electric seal are cheap but useful substitutes. The former is made from the skins of Belgian rabbits, and the latter from those of French rabbits. Coney seal is best, and a coat of good quality can be secured for £15. After all, imitation has been described as the sincerest form of flattery.

A NEEDLEWORK BOARD

A LITTLE work-board provides one of the most compact and convenient methods of carrying the implements and materials required for sewing when travelling. In order to make this, ask a carpenter to cut a small board 8 inches square and ⅜ of an inch thick. Cover this with a pretty shade of Nattier blue cloth, securing it in place with small tacks along the under edge. Cut a piece of cloth medium shade 9 by 11½ inches for the cover, and either have it pinked around the edge or buttonhole it with silk. This should be fixed with a few tacks on the under part of the board at the upper edge.

Now make a small pincushion measuring 3 inches by 2 inches. Cover it with cloth and put a fancy buttonhole stitch around the edge. Fix this in the centre of the board at the top, with a little brass-headed nail at each corner. Cut a needle book-cover of the cloth 3 inches long by 2½ inches wide. Buttonhole it with silk around the edge. Make two little leaves of white delaine with snipped edges. Put these level

An attractive and useful needlework board which can be made easily at home

with the cover and turn the edge of the cover over them at the top, and nail it to the board in the left-hand corner with three brass-headed nails. Get four reels of cotton, a 30 and a 60, in black and white. Put long brass-headed screws through them, and attach them to the board, two on each side of the little pincushion.

Then get a little fancy metal box, make a hole in the middle, and screw it down in the centre of the board. This is for holding a yard measure. Below this is an elastic for the thimble, and in the right-hand lower corner another elastic for the bodkin and scissors. When this is done, cover the underneath of the board with a piece of dark-coloured sateen, and oversew it around the edges.

It looks best to have the buttonholing done in a colour which contrasts with the cloth.

Cost: 4d. for the board, 4d. for the cottons, 6d. for the little box, and another 6d. for the scissors, and 1d. for the thimble. Total: 2s. 7d. Value of board: 5s. 6d. or 6s.

DRESS IN THE STUART PERIOD

A SOURCE OF INSPIRATION TO MODERN DESIGNERS

By MARY HOWARTH

How Hints for the same Dress may be picked up from several Old Pictures—The large Hats worn by Nell Gwynn—Cavaliers and their Rich Clothing—Patches and Chopines

THE Stuart period serves, in the history of dress as well as politically, as a dividing line between modes ancient and modern. It was essentially a period of transition. The destruction of the Spanish Armada one regards as ancient history (although people still syndicate themselves for the purpose of discovering wrecked galleons), but the adventures of Bonnie Prince Charlie appeal to one as a romance of modern times. Similarly, it is with a realisation of comparative modernity that one contemplates the fashion of patching the face, whilst the Elizabethan ruff seems to be a relic of almost prehistoric times.

Art as a Source of Inspiration

Designers of dress find their best inspiration in old pictures, taking from this one a slashed sleeve, from another a rosetted belt, from a third a panier, and from a fourth a short-waisted corsage cut in battlements. Among the most potent sources of aid are the portraits painted during the reigns of the Stuart kings and the dominion of the Protectorate, when men and women elected to be sent down to posterity clad in their best, the Royalists in all the finery of their brave array, the Puritans in the sober guise it satisfied their consciences to wear. The great Dutch portrait painters, Sir Anthony Van Dyck, commonly known as Vandyke, and Sir Peter Lely, have left us an absolutely faithful delineation of fashion in this most interesting of periods. Their portraits of the Kings Charles I. and Charles II., and of their queens and their renowned favourites, and of Oliver Cromwell are a running comment on the modes of a day that has come down to posterity as a byword for extravagance in every way.

The contemporary period in France was just as rich in superb habiliments, and the portraiture of that period is a gold-mine to the

King Charles I. led the fashion for extravagant attire. In this picture by Vandyke he is seen with the Star of the Garter blazing on his cloak, and in his ear a beautiful pearl drop.

clever conjurer in clothes, for it must be admitted that with the world as old as it is now, novelty worthy of the name is rare, and any originality in dress can usually be traced to bygone days. Certain deft alterations have, of course, to be made, for fashion never repeats herself slavishly. She would be her own undoing were she to be so unwise.

Mignard's Madonnas

The name of the great court artist Mignard is closely associated with the grand ladies of his day in France, at which time his style was so admired that the ladies he did not paint were as anxious as if he had painted them to be distinguished as the possessors of "mignard" faces, "mignard" expressions of countenance, and even of "mignard" smiles. All Mignard's sitters were madonnas.

Much mirthful criticism has been expressed of late respecting the fashions of the twentieth century. But our large hats, copied from the stupendous millinery worn by the charming Nell Gwynn, and even our hobble skirts, are the meekest and mildest of freaks compared with some of the exaggerations in which the madcaps of the seventeenth century indulged.

James I. himself led the way towards the goal of sheer and foolish eccentricity by wearing clothing so distended by padding that he looked like a figure of fun, the "Punch" of that and other generations. There was method in the sovereign's madness, we are told, for he suffered so much from fear of assassination that he desired to make his attire dagger-proof, and thus took advantage of the fashion that had arisen in Queen Elizabeth's day for copious stuffings, which gave an overblown appearance to everyone.

It must be remembered that during this

period men hankered after the moral support of stupendously rich clothing. Their taste for splendid apparel provided a subject very much to the taste of the Roundheads, who went to the opposite extreme in the matter of wearing plain and sober clothing, and spared no one the scathing of bitterest criticism.

To enumerate some of the evidences of this strange masculine love for the fal-lals and fripperies of dress, there is the satirist Henry FitzGeoffery's record of a " spruce coxcombe "

" That never walkes without his looking-glasse
In a tobacco box or diall set
That he may privately confere with it."

Suits of pure white silk velvet were a favourite extravagance, with just one touch of colour in the scarlet heels of the white leather shoes and the relieving hint of black provided by the gloves. Men wore stays, "whale-bone bodyes" they were styled; they cherished one or two long lovelocks, which hung far below their flowing hair, perched gorgeous bows on their shoes, known as shoe roses, wore shoulder knots, carried muffs, and hung jewels in their ears. There is a superb portrait of Charles I., reticent, aloof, melancholy, and proud, with the Star of the Garter blazing on his cloak and in his ear a beautiful pearl drop. What wonder is it that plays based on the period are so decorative, and that for fancy dress balls the " spruce coxcombes " of to-day choose to impersonate the lordly Royalists of the past.

Catherine of Braganza, the beautiful Queen of Charles II., wearing the ringlets, jewels, and superbly-elaborate costume of the period.

It was only natural that the " mincing madams " of the period elected to outshine the men if possible, and vied with them to introduce strange wonders into their schemes of apparel. They were light-hearted butterflies by nature, and had the wit to appear so even when tears would have been more grateful to them than smiles ; for merry-making was à la mode. It was a profession of faith and of politics to turn a mocking face to fortune, or the inference was that the stern creed of Puritanism had clutched them.

To which fashion should the palm for foolishness be given—that for wearing chopines or for patching the face ? We of this day are, of course, most interested in patches, for from time to time there is a threatening of the old epidemic, and a little crescent, or round dot, accentuating the curve of a lip or the whiteness of a forehead causes the alarmist to foretell a return of the strange custom of literally plastering the face

with devices, such as stars, moons, suns, a mourning coach and horses, and so forth.

The chopine, or chapiney, was a species of clog or false heel, rising so high in some instances that it merited the title stilt. This originated in Turkey, enjoyed a vogue in Venice, and thence came to England.

Made of wood covered with leather in such colours as red or yellow, while some were altogether white, the chopines were worn under the shoes, raising their wearers in some instances to as great a height as half a yard, in which case the devotees of the absurd contrivance had to be supported when they walked.

Stigmatised as a monstrous affectation, chopines were made the subject of satire in many a play. Hamlet alludes to them in the line, "Your ladyship is nearer heaven than when I saw you last by the altitude of a chopine."

As for the fancy for patching the face, it came into vogue at the close of the reign of Charles I., and, despite the check of the Commonwealth, which held in subjection many a fashionable vagary, maintained its popularity down to the reign of Queen Anne, when the position occupied by the patches indicated the politics of the wearers.

It is said that there was a reasonable excuse for wearing patches when first they were introduced, for that they were plasters prescribed as a remedy for headache. Be that as it may, one of the polite arts of the period was to patch the face with due effect, and in the middle of the promenade great ladies would stop, open their patch boxes, survey themselves in the looking-glass which lined the lid, and if there was any repair to make, carry it out.

Pictures of the seventeenth century show the fine ladies of the Court in their satin dresses, wearing huge sleeves ruffled with lace, a rather short-waisted bodice with a battlemented basque, and a belt finished with a rosette at the side (now being copied for the autumnal frock), also a very large and graceful cambric collar edged with a double frill of exquisite lace. Some of the fair ones carry muffs, and wear fur stoles and tippets, whilst others cling to their fans. Very many of them are masked.

This wearing of masks is a very interesting item in the history of costume which will be dealt with in our next article.

To be continued.

The following are good firms for supplying materials, etc., mentioned in this Section : Messrs. Grenfell, Frazier & Co. (Jewellery). Horrockses' Longcloths and Sheetings (Wholesale only), London Glove Co. (Gloves)

D 30   I C

WOMAN'S DRESS

Conducted by the Editress of " Fashions for All "

In this important section of EVERY WOMAN'S ENCYCLOPÆDIA every aspect of dress will be dealt with by practical and experienced writers. The history of dress from earliest times will be told, and practical and useful information will be given in :

Home Dressmaking

How to Cut Patterns
Methods of Self-measurement
Colour Contrasts

Home Tailoring
Representative Fashions
Fancy Dress
Alteration of Clothes, etc.

Millinery

Lessons in Hat Trimming
How to Make a Shape
How to Curl Feathers
Flowers, Hat-pins, Colours, etc.

Boots and Shoes

Choice
How to Keep in Good Condition
How to Soften Leather, etc.

Furs

Choice
How to Preserve, etc.
How to Detect Frauds

Gloves

Choice
Cleaning, etc.

Jewellery, etc.

PRACTICAL ADVICE ON THE CHOICE OF FURS

By THE HON. MRS. FITZROY STEWART

Continued from page 383, Part 3

No. 4. ERMINE

The Royal and Judicial Fur—The Ermine of Commerce—Habits and Characteristics of the Animal—Its Decorative Effects—The History of Ermine as a Decoration to Regal and Official Dress—Its Use in Early Times

ERMINE is a Royal and judicial fur ; but, with us, sumptuary laws have long ceased to exist. It is one of the furs of heraldry, and is worn by the King and Queen, by judges, and on the State robes of peers and of certain high officials.

The Characteristics of the Animal

The ermine of commerce is taken from a species of stoat, which wears a white dress during the winter season. It has a body about 10 inches long and 2½ inches wide, and its tail is about 4 inches in length. It has the short legs and the slender body of the weasel—its poor relation. And, like others of its species, it is a small, restless, and—one must add—bloodthirsty animal.

The ermine preys on birds, rabbits, and other small creatures, and, although useful in destroying rats and mice, is a sworn foe to the poultry-yard.

It moves with great quickness, climbs trees well, swims easily, and makes its home among rocks, stones, and other rough surroundings. It wears a brown coat in summer, and changes to pure white in winter, with the exception of its nose, tail, and whiskers, which always remain black. In snowy regions the protective value of this white fur is obvious ; and that the change occurs in connection with a lowered temperature seems certain, although the physiology of the process is not as yet understood. The creature breeds at the end of winter, and, like a cat, carries its young by the nape of the neck into a place of safety.

How and Where it is Caught

The ermine is distributed in the northern parts of Europe, Asia, and America, but has been found as far south as the Italian Alps and the Pyrenees. Its movements are rapid, and its capture is beset with difficulty. Moreover, it is shy and wary and hard to trap, since only a jet-black tail is visible as the little animal flits across the expanse of snowfields. The trapper often makes his lure of twigs of wood, the smallest of steel traps being too heavy for the best specimens.

A hunter will often put grease on his hunting-knife, and lay it down on the trails of the ermine. And when the little white form appears the grease attracts it, and it licks the blade of the knife, only to find that its tiny tongue is frozen hard to the ice-cold steel, that the knife is too heavy to move, and that its frantic struggles to escape are useless. One can only hope that the hunter puts the poor creature at once out of its misery.

Ermine skins are imported from Norway, Lapland, Siberia, and the Hudson Bay Territory, but the best skins come from Siberia. The choicest ermine is soft and pure white, and a fine skin costs from £1 upwards. The skins that have a yellowish tinge are far less valuable. In fact, the price depends on colour and quality, and therefore fluctuates considerably.

The Value of the Fur

Good ermine rose to a high price in 1902, and is likely to be valuable again in 1911. A long coat of the best ermine now costs from £250 to £300 ; a long stole, about £100 ; a short tie, from £8 to £14 ; and a big muff, from £15 to £25. Real tails are used to trim the best ermine, but for the cheaper sort the tails are imitated by means of bits of dark fur taken from the skunk or the squirrel.

Ermine has been the Royal fur of England since the time of Edward III., who forbade its use by anyone who was not of blood royal. And there was a law in Austria to the same effect, which has remained in force up to the present period.

Our Royal ermine, known as miniver, must have a word of explanation. Strictly speaking, this fur is the pure white skin of the Siberian miniver squirrel, but the name is also applied to ermine when unvaried by the usual black tail tips. In either case, the spots required are made from Persian lamb or from sealskin. If from the former, they are tiny morsels of silky fur obtained from between the toes of the black lamb ; but sealskin is invariably used for the best miniver. For instance, an expert declares that ten thousand small bits of sealskin will be worked into the miniver which will line the cloak of King George V. on the day of his Coronation.

Ermine as the Emblem of Rank

Again, the Royal crown is bordered with a band of ermine, with one row of black spots. Ermine, moreover, plays a big part in the robes and coronets of peers and peeresses. Their coronets have a band of spotted ermine, and ermine appears on their robes according to their place in the peerage. A duke's crimson velvet mantle is edged with miniver, and the cape is furred with miniver, having four rows of dark spots on each shoulder. A duchess will have the cape of her crimson velvet mantle furred with miniver, five inches in breadth, and varied (" powdered " is the correct term) by four bars or rows of ermine. A marquis's robes have but three and a half bars of ermine, and a marchioness has but three and a half bars of ermine and a miniver edging, which is reduced to four inches in breadth. An earl's mantle is distinguished from the preceding by having but three bars of ermine, and his countess has on her cape only three inches of miniver. And the scale descends, as a viscount and viscountess

have only two and a half rows of ermine ; and a baron and baroness must content themselves with only two bars of this fur, and with but a bare two inches of miniver edging.

Ermine is light in weight, wears well, and will stand repeated cleanings, but it has one grave fault : it is fatally easy to imitate. There is no material used in articles of dress in which fraud is so frequent as in furs, nor in which there is such ample scope for cheating.

Unless a woman has special knowledge, she is entirely at the mercy of her furrier. Sham ermine is made from shorn and prepared white rabbit skins, or from white fur taken from the lower part of the squirrel. But the fraud can be easily detected, as the best rabbit skin will not bear comparison with the poorest ermine. In the case of imitation fur the hair is soft, and will soon wear at the edges, and it has none of the fineness and gloss of real ermine. And tails are seen as mere strips of curled black fur upon even a slight examination.

An Unbecoming Fur

In this relation it may be said that the Chamber of Commerce issued a warning to the public, through the Press, as to the misnaming of furs, giving the names of certain furs and their incorrect descriptions. At the same time the chamber sent out to the wholesale and retail fur warehouses a list of " permissible descriptions." In this list sham ermine appears as follows : " Proper name—white rabbit. Incorrect—ermine. Permissible—mock ermine." But the " permissible descriptions " have few defenders, as the actual name of the animal is, in most cases, not mentioned.

Ermine has beauty, but it is one of the most unbecoming furs in existence. The effect is hard and crude, and the dead white proves a trial even to the fairest complexion. Ermine is much worn by smart Parisians, especially in the spring and early autumn. But Frenchwomen are artists, and tone down the effect by means of lace, tulle, or chiffon. Ermine is at its best when worn with dark-coloured velvets. The contrast of a black velvet or deep violet velvet gown with ermine makes a perfect *ensemble*.

Suitable for Evening Wear

Ermine looks well in the evening. It can be worn as a stole for the shoulders, or as a long cloak, which has a regal effect; or else to line a cloak of satin or velvet.

Ermine, however, has a third fault, it does not combine well with other furs, but stands aloof in its proud purity. One often sees it mixed with musquash or sealskin, but a woman of fine taste finds the sharp colour contrast a trifle hard and aggressive. Ermine mates best with moleskin, and an ermine tie and muff worn with a moleskin coat will show to immense advantage.

Ermine is a fur that adapts itself well to small articles and trimmings. In fact, one wonders that it is not more often used to trim Court trains and wedding costumes. A winter bride does wisely who has her white velvet train trimmed with ermine. And this has had a precedent. When the beautiful Miss Enid Wilson became Lady Chesterfield, she wore a white velvet Court train bordered with ermine, and made a fairy tale bride on a snowy February morning in 1900.

When before-Easter Courts are again in vogue, fine effects might be produced with ermine on white satin, brocade, or velvet. Contrasts of texture, rather than of colour, have much interest. Whistler's symphony in white makes a good example ; and a more modern instance is that of a young duchess who once wore her famous pearls with a cream costume. Ermine, well arranged, has many possibilities.

Its Ancient Popularity

The fur was known to the ancients, and owed its début to the Byzantine emperors. The Greeks, who were fond of ermine, believed it to be the skin of the white rat, and Wagner was the first naturalist to class the creature among the weasels. The Byzantines called it the Armenian rat fur ; hence the words Hermine and ermine ; and until late in the seventeenth century it was called *le rat d'Arménie*.

In old days the finest skins were obtained from the rich plateau of the Taurus (Armenia). And even now the great ermine markets of the world are at Van, Erivan, and Mitlis. But the creature was found elsewhere, as the Dukes of Brittany used to wear ermine robes of native production. Marco Polo, in his book of travels, mentions ermine as among the most costly dress of the Tartars ; and remarks that he found the tents of the Cham of Tartary lined with the skins of ermine and sables in the year 1252.

Ermine does not appear to have been used as an official mark of distinction earlier than the fourth century ; and in the fifth it was adopted by the French as a sign of legal dignity. This custom still remains, as the judges have their scarlet robes edged with ermine. It was also used at a very early age by the Court of Rome for the State garments

of the cardinals ; but the little black tails were usually omitted in church costumes, in order to emphasise the purity of the priestly profession.

Then, in later times, one Czar of Russia had Coronation robes, in the making of which 250,000 ermines were sacrificed ; and the Coronation robes of the first Napoleon, preserved at Notre Dame, are also lined with the most costly ermine.

Ermine Makes History

The earlier Queens of the House of Hanover were especially fond of narrow stripes of ermine, perhaps to emphasise their regal dignity. The hanging sleeves affected by Queen Charlotte are often seen lined with black-tailed ermine; and there is a good portrait of Queen Adelaide with a deep ermine tippet. The Duchess of Kent, too, is represented as wearing a round cape of ermine And the Coronation robes of Queen Victoria and of our late King Edward were splendid specimens of the art of the furrier. Ermine is a fur that makes history.

Ermine is a fur that must be treated with due care and consideration. Its fine quality and pure whiteness causes it to become easily soiled and damaged. A careful lady's-maid would wrap her mistress's ermine fur in layers of tissue paper ; and, after use, a muff, stole, or necktie should be lightly wiped over with a fine white cloth— for choice, with a cambric handkerchief. A brush must never be used, and, if wet, ermine must not be dried by the fire, but should be gently shaken.

Photo, Reutlinger

Ermine worn as a cloak has a regal effect, the black tails forming the most suitable trimming. A stole of the fur, with tails at the ends, is another favourite arrangement of ermine

And even when economy is an object, good fur should be sent, when soiled, to a furrier's, and by no means be subjected to what is known as "home-cleaning." And precious fur of any sort ought never to be left in a room with a dog, unguarded. A tragic tale is told of a costly ermine muff worried to pieces in its owner's absence.

PRACTICAL LESSONS IN DRESSMAKING

Continued from page 379, Part 3

By M. PRINCE BROWNE

Examiner in Dressmaking, Tailoring, French Pattern Modelling, Plain Needlework, and Millinery, of the Teachers in Training at the University College of South Wales and Monmouthshire, Cardiff; the London Higher Technical Examination Centres, etc.; First Class Diploma for Tailoring; Diploma of Honour for Dressmaking; Diploma of Merit of the Highest Order for Teaching; Silver Medallist, London Exhibition, 1900; Silver Medal, Franco-British Exhibition, 1908; Author of " Up-to-Date Dresscutting and Drafting," also " The Practical Work of Dressmaking and Tailoring."

FOURTH LESSON. FANCY STITCHES—*continued*

Honeycombing—Smocking—Cross-stitch—French Knots

Honeycombing

HONEYCOMBING is an ornamental stitch sometimes used instead of gathering to contract the fulness of any part of a garment to the size desired. It is more generally used for children's garments, but sometimes it is used for blouses, etc. When finished, the work has the appearance of rows of diamond-shaped cells united by dots, and looks somewhat like a section of honeycomb.

The amount of material required for the fulness is about double the width the honeycombing is to be when finished. The diamonds forming the honeycomb must always be kept *regular and even*.

To prepare the work, spread the piece of material to be worked smoothly on a table or board—wrong side uppermost—stretch a tape measure straight across it, and pin it firmly down at each end with a drawing-pin. Take a finely pointed pencil, and make a dot at each half-inch—more or less—all along the portion of material to be honeycombed. Make a succession of horizontal rows of dots half an inch apart—more or less—to the depth the honeycombing is to be worked.

N.B.—The dots *must* be accurately and lightly marked on to the material, or the work will not be a success.

Paper ready marked with dots can be bought—for a few pence—at any fancy shop, and the dots can be transferred to the material by means of a warm iron.

To do this, cut the paper to the required size, place it face downwards on the wrong side of the material, and press all over it with a warm iron.

When the paper is removed the dots should appear on the material; but, as this paper is only made with blue and orange-coloured dots, it is better in most cases for the worker herself to lightly pencil the dots on to the material. The work is next prepared for the honeycombing by running a tacking-cotton along each line of dots—from right to left—taking up on the needle and passing over half of the space between each dot, as shown in diagram 1.

When all the horizontal lines of dots have been run in this way, draw up all the threads closely and evenly, stick a pin into the material at the end of each row, and twist the tacking-thread round it three or four times to prevent it slipping.

Commence the work at top right-hand corner, and *oversew* the first and second gathers together two or three times—according to the size the dot is to be made and the thickness of the silk with which it is being worked. Slip the needle down inside the fold of the second gather to the

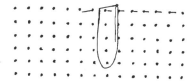

Diagram 1. Dots marked on material ready for honeycombing. Run a tacking-thread along each line of dots

row *below*, and oversew the *second* and *third* gathers together, with the same number of stitches as in the first dot. Slip the needle *inside* the fold of the third, gather up to the *top* row, and oversew the *third* and *fourth* gathers together—with the same number of stitches—so that all the dots may match. Continue to work in the same way to the end of the first two rows. Commence the third and fourth rows, and work them in the same way as the first and second, taking up the same gathers in the *third* row as in the *first*, and the same gathers in the *fourth* as in the *second* row.

Work the remainder of the rows in this way, making every alternate one match, then take out the tacking-threads.

Smocking

Smocking is prepared in the same way as honeycombing, but as the stitches are not so elastic, more material is required for it. The amount to be allowed for the fulness is about two and a half or three times—according to the thickness of the material—the width the smocking is to be when finished.

The stitches used are embroidery, herring-bone, and featherstitch, as well as cable, basket, rope, etc., and these are worked *across* the gathers, after they have been prepared in the same way as described for honeycombing.

Smocking is largely used for children's frocks, etc., as it is picturesque; and the tops and sleeves of blouses are frequently smocked.

Cross-stitch

Cross-stitch, as used in dressmaking, is an ornamental method of sewing in the tight band of a bodice, also of marking the centre of the skirt-band.

To work the cross for the latter, place a pin at the centre of the front of the band, thread a needle with twist—to match that used to "fan" the bones of the bodice—make a knot, and from the wrong side bring the needle through near the top of the band, about one-eighth of an inch to the left of the pin. Stick the needle through to the wrong side, near the bottom of the band, and about one-eighth of an inch to the right of the pin ; draw it through, and bring it up again to the right side near the bottom of the band, and about one-eighth of an inch to the *left* of the pin.

Put the needle in near the top of the band, about one-eighth of an inch to the *right* of the pin, and draw the twist through. This should form a cross on the right side. As this cross should be thick, work the stitches over *in the same places* about three times. Take out the pin, and work two or three short, straight stitches over the centre of the cross, to secure it in position. To work the cross-stitch to fix the "tight band" into a bodice, work the stitch in the same way, but pass the needle *each* time *under* the bone, so as to secure the band firmly to the bodice. The "tight band" in the back of the bodice is necessary to draw it well down, so that the back may set smoothly on the wearer.

French Knots

French knots, or, as this stitch is sometimes called, knot-stitch, is frequently used in conjunction with feather-stitching to make it still more ornamental ; also in white and coloured embroidery, to form stamens in working daisies, and other flowers, etc. To work the stitch, thread a needle with cotton, twist, or whatever is to be used for working the knots ; make a knot at the end, and bring the needle through to the right side of the work ; hold the thread in the left hand, an inch or two from the material, and, holding the needle in the right hand, twist it round the thread three or four times—according to the size the knot is to be and the thickness of the thread with which it is being worked—twist the needle *over* the thread to the left, and *under* it to the right, still holding the thread firmly in the left hand ; stick the needle into the work *close* to the place where the thread was first drawn through, and hold the twists of thread in their place with the left thumb, whilst drawing the needle and thread through to the wrong side. Pull the thread tight, to secure the knot firmly.

Diagram 2. How to work French knots, a most decorative stitch used in dressmaking

Another method of working the knot-stitch is to draw the needle up from the wrong side, hold the working thread between the thumb and first finger of the left hand, and twist it twice round the needle—*over* it to the left, *under* it to the right.

Turn the needle round from left to right, and form a back-stitch by sticking it into the material a few threads beyond where the thread was first drawn through, and up again a few threads in front of it. While holding down the two stitches that are on the needle with the left thumb, draw the needle and thread through gently, ready for the next stitch. Care must be taken not to pucker the material by drawing the thread too tightly between the knots. The knots must all be firm and evenly worked, and when working upon double material the needle should always be slipped *between* in passing from one stitch to another, so that the wrong side of the work may also look neat.

To be continued.

PRACTICAL LESSONS IN TAILORING
FOR HOME WORKERS AND OTHERS
By M. PRINCE BROWNE

Examiner in Dressmaking, Tailoring, French Pattern Modelling, Millinery, and Plain Needlework of the Teachers in Training at the University College of South Wales and Monmouthshire, Cardiff, the London Technical Examination Centre, etc. Author of " Up-to-Date Dresscutting and Drafting," also " The Practical Work of Dressmaking and Tailoring."

Continued from page 380, Part 3

FOURTH LESSON. POCKETS—*continued*

Flap Pocket—Patch Pocket—Circular Pocket

Flap Pocket—*continued*

FASTEN off the threads of the four ends of the stitching firmly, pull each thread through, and tie it to its own under-thread ; but on no account must the threads of the upper and lower row of stitching be tied together. Take a small, short, sharp pair of scissors, and cut carefully between the two rows of stitching ; cut from the centre to each end, but not beyond, or there will be a hole in the coat at each end of the flap. If the space between the stitching will allow of it, the cut at each end can be made slightly slanting almost to meet each row of stitching, thus leaving a tiny tongue of the cloth at each end —this little tongue is made in order that the corners may set perfectly flat when turned in—but if the rows of stitching are too close

38

together for the opening to be cut in this way, it is not only unnecessary, but cannot be done. The lower of the two pieces of lining must now be passed through the opening and tacked down quite close to the turning—the lining and cloth being level at the edge. A row of machine stitching should then be placed as near as possible to the edge of this turning.

The upper piece of lining must now be passed through the opening—the flap only being left on the right side.

The small seam which attaches the flap to the coat must next be pressed open, and as flat as possible, and a row of machine stitching worked on the coat just above the flap, and close to the seam. This row of stitching must correspond with the one which is round the edge of the flap—if there are two rows of stitching round the flap, there must be two rows at the top; and the second of these must be continued down each end, to appear as if it continued beneath the flap. The two pieces of lining which are to form the pocket must be tacked together and stitched round, without, of course, taking any stitches through to the coat. A small piece of linen must be placed and pinned at each end of the opening, on the wrong side of the coat, and over the pocket just made.

The small tongue of the material which is on the right side must be turned in with a strong needle, and firmly fastened down by a sort of felling stitch.

This is done by prodding the needle up and down, passing it from the wrong side (through the small piece of linen) up close to the turned-in edge of the tongue, and down again well under the edge, so that no stitch is visible on the right side. As many of these stitches as are necessary must be made at each end of the pocket. These ends must not be puckered, and great care must be taken to make them lie perfectly flat, and not to show beyond the flap.

N.B.—If the pocket has been properly made the flap, if passed into the pocket, should lie quite flat without the opening showing beyond it at either side.

The pocket must be well pressed (on the wrong side) with a tailor's goose.

When finished, the right side of this pocket should appear as in diagram No. 1, and the wrong side as in diagram No. 2.

Patch Pocket

A patch pocket is simply a piece of the same cloth as the coat or other garment being made, or a piece of the lining—if the pocket is to be inside and the coat or other garment is to be lined—cut to the desired shape and size and turned in and tacked all round. Before the pocket is put on, the top edge must be finished off by being turned in and " faced " with lute ribbon or Prussian binding; or turned in and " faced " to the lining (if there is one), and one or more rows of machine stitching may be worked across, if desired.

It must then be well pressed, tacked on to the garment, and either machine stitched or sewn on by hand, if the stitches must not show through.

Circular Pocket

The method of making the circular pocket can be learned (as in the case of the flap pocket) on a piece of cloth. To make the pocket take a piece of tailor's chalk, and on the right side of the cloth draw a slightly curved line about $4\frac{1}{2}$ or 5 inches across, as illustrated in diagram No. 3. Cut a piece of linen about $5\frac{1}{4}$ or 6 inches long, selvedge - wise, and about $2\frac{1}{4}$ inches wide; place this on the wrong side of the piece of cloth, exactly under the curved line (which is drawn on the right side), leaving an equal length of the linen beyond the end of the line on each side; pin it in this position, and tack the cloth to the linen ; the tacking must be done on the right side exactly on and along the chalk line, so that the line of tacking stitches on the wrong side exactly reproduces the chalk line on the right side.

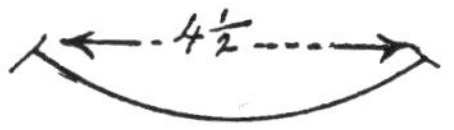

N.B.—This straight piece of linen is to strengthen the opening of the pocket, and to prevent it stretching.

Cut a piece of the same cloth slightly longer than the chalk line, about 3 inches wide, and exactly on the cross; place it right side downwards " facing " the piece of cloth in which the pocket is being made, over the chalk line, leaving (as near as possible) an equal amount of the crossway piece beyond it all round, and pin it in this position.

N.B.—If the material is diagonal, the crossway piece must be cut across the diagonal lines, and not with them. Turn the work over and, from the wrong side, tack on the

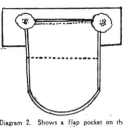

Diagram 1. A flap pocket as it should appear on the right side of coat

Diagram 2. Shows a flap pocket on the wrong side

Diagram 3. Draw a slightly curved line in tailor's chalk on the right side of material piece of cloth, following the curved line of tacking stitches already made.

This should reproduce the curved line on the crossway piece.

Take a piece of tailor's chalk and correct this line, so that the curve may be quite perfect before the stitching is done. Machine-stitch on each side of the line, but not round the corners.

Commence and cut off the thread at the end of each line.

The space between the two lines of stitching must depend upon the cloth—if it

Diagram 4. Tack the two edges together from left to right, and back again from right to left

is not likely to fray, the lines of stitching can be worked very near together, just allowing for the opening for the pocket to be cut between them ; but if it is not a closely woven material they must be further apart. However, the closer the lines can be stitched, the better the pocket will appear when the work is finished.

N.B.—The space between the two lines of stitching must be the same all along the curve, and both lines must be exactly the same length.

The upper thread at each of the four ends must be drawn through and tied firmly to its own under-thread, but they must never be tied across the ends.

The opening must now be made for the pocket. Take a small, short, sharp pair of scissors, and cut carefully between the

two rows of stitching ; cut from the centre to each end as far as the stitching, but not beyond. If the space between the stitching will allow of it, the cut at each end can be made slightly slanting, almost to meet each row of stitching, thus leaving a tiny tongue of the cloth at each end ; this little tongue is made in order that the corners may set perfectly flat when turned in. But if the rows of stitching are too close together for the opening to be cut in this way, it is not only unnecessary, but cannot be done. Turn the crossway piece of cloth through the opening to the wrong side, and tack it closely all round, and quite near to the edge of it—this should give the opening the appearance of being corded, and not bound round ; the corners must set quite smoothly, and not appear puckered. Tack the two edges together, passing the needle through the corded edge only, tacking over and over, from left to right, and back again from right to left, drawing the two edges together just to meet, but not to overlap, and forming a cross-stitch, as shown in diagram No. 4.

Place the work wrong side uppermost on a bare sleeve or ironing board, cover it with a cloth, well wrung out of water, and press it well with a tailor's goose. Place one or more rows of machine stitching round the opening near the edge.

N.B.—In making a coat, the pocket is the first part which is to be stitched (for ornament), and as the number of rows placed on it must correspond with those to be placed round the collar, revers, etc., the number must be decided upon before the pocket is stitched.

To be continued.

PRACTICAL MILLINERY
By Mrs. ERIC PRITCHARD

Continued from page 377, Part 3

Fur as a Season's Trimming—The Combination of Fur and Lace—The Intricacies of Rosette-making

WE must always remember that no hard-and-fast rules can be laid down with regard to the trimming of headgear. Every season has its novelty—or, rather, many novelties—but the best *modistes* of the world never overtrim their models, but depend rather on the application of fabrics of good quality at an artistic angle on the shape itself. The amateur, however, has much to learn regarding the elementary laws of trimming, even admitting that she has mastered in some degree the difficulty of shape-making and covering. In the last article we rehearsed the phases of tying the simplest bows ; in this we will further elaborate a popular trimming.

Fur is used on hats no less than on dresses, and on millinery it is light and elegant as an edging to the lace rosette ; a wintry appearance is therefore given to the hat without overloading the shape in a physical or an artistic sense, though, of course, fur is used equally for velvet or silk bows. It is sold by the leading drapers in strips, from 3s. 11½d. a yard, for millinery purposes ;

marabout strips are also used, where a lighter and cheaper edging is required. For the lace bow, 1 yard of guipure or torchon lace, in black or white, at 2s. 11½d. per yard, 18 inches wide, and 4 yards of skunk or marabout will be required.

To Make the Bow

Fig. 1

Take 36 inches of lace, and cut it in half lengthways. This will give two lengths, each 36 inches by 9 inches.

Fig. 2

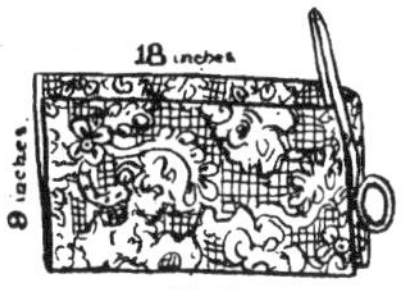

Fig 8

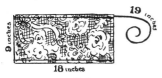

Fig. 3

Cut each of these lengths in half; this gives four lengths, each 18 by 9 inches. Three pieces are for the loops and the fourth for the "tie-over."

Take the third length and sew on one inch from the top right-side front of bow, but on the slant; this is to avoid stiffness. Bend the wire here and there to give a softer effect.

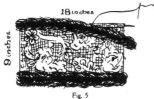

Fig. 4

Hem the two long sides of each piece, and leave the hem sufficiently wide to allow a wire to be inserted.

Nip off eight lengths of wire, each measuring 19 inches. Then push one of these through each hem separately to support and strengthen the bow.

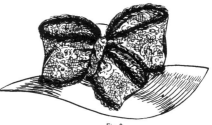

Fig. 9

Sew the bow on to the left-side front of hat, and stitch through the crown.

Tie or knot, as artistically as possible, the remaining piece of lace over centre.

A large rosette of Chantilly lace edged with skunk would also be a very smart finish for a hat. If skunk is too expensive, marabout or a velvet edging can be substituted.

Rosette-making

For a fairly large rosette, 1 yard of Chantilly lace, black or white, 18 inches wide (about 2s. 11½d. per yard), 5 yards of skunk or marabout, or any other fur selected, and two rings of lace wire to support the lace, are necessary.

Fig. 5

Sew an edging of fur along each hem, on the wrong side, being careful not to catch the hair.

Fig. 10

Fig. 6

Make loops of three lengths, as illustrated, and pleat each at the ends.

Cut lace in half lengthways; this gives two lengths, 36 by 9 inches each. The first stages are the same as described above for the making of the bow.

Fig. 7

Join two of these lengths together.

Fig. 11

41

Fold one of the lengths in half, then re-fold and cut, leaving four pieces, each 9 by 9 inches (see Fig. 11).

9 inches

Fig. 12

Repeat the same with other half, and there will then be eight separate pieces, or squares, 9 by 9 inches each.

4 inches

Fig. 16

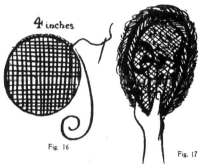

Fig. 17

Pin all the squares one on the top of the other, round off each square at the top; this gives eight leaves, as illustrated. The object of placing one on the other is to secure perfect uniformity of curve.

Fig. 13

Pleat one of the leaves at foot with thumb and forefinger, and sew on to the edge of an ear, one inch down.

The leaves, or loops, must now be supported by wire. Hem each leaf very neatly, and leave the hem sufficiently wide to allow the wire to pass. Push wire through the hem.

Fig. 14

Fig. 15

Sew the fur round each leaf, remembering to take up only the extreme edge of the fur.

The leaves are now ready, and we come to the most difficult part of the task, which is to put the leaves artistically together so as to form a rosette. It is almost impossible to describe how to do this, for the result depends on the worker's own discretion and taste.

Commence by taking a small piece of stiff net or buckram, or anything stiff in black (if black lace is used), cut out a circle 4 inches in diameter.

Buttonhole-stitch the wire round, or double lace wire could be used if no ordinary wire is obtainable (see Fig. 15).

It is as well to remember exactly how to make these rounds, as they are continually being required for trimming. The technical term for them in millinery is " ears," and the *modiste* uses them as a foundation for mounting and supporting feathers, bows, flowers, etc. ; but this is a point requiring special skill.

Fig. 18

Sew five leaves round the outer circle of this ear, each pleated in the same way.

The remaining three leaves are to be used for filling in the centre, and here again individual taste is the worker's guide.

Fig. 19. The hat complete

Fig. 19 illustrates the rosette completed, with a small piece of fur, or a cabuchon ornament, placed in the centre to finish it off neatly, and sewn in position on the hat.

The edge of each leaf is straight, but the wire can be bent and curved according to taste, to render the effect as artistic as possible.

42

LACE SCARVES

The many Uses and Value of Real Lace Scarves—An ideal Wedding Present—Such Scarves may be Worn on the Shoulders, as Fichus, as Mantillas, or as Hoods

AMONG those dainty dress accessories which are always graceful and never out of date, long scarves of filmy lace must hold a place of honour. Many a portrait painter owes to them a deep debt of gratitude, for they have come to his aid times without number, softening the angles in some instances, and in others concealing an exuberance of outline with equal amiability.

For wearers of all ages, too, the lace scarf can be successfully adapted, since it may serve appropriately as a baby's christening veil or as a head-dress for baby's grandmother, who will be well advised to bring the long ends round under her chin, and to fasten them with some quaint old-world brooch set possibly with garnets and seed pearls.

A long and fairly wide scarf of fine real lace is a possession of which any woman may be proud. In the present, for her own use it has infinite possibilities, and in the future she likes to think that it will be handed down as an heirloom for generations to come.

When, therefore, rich aunts and fairy godmothers are debating as to their choice of wedding presents, let them always remember that a long lace scarf makes an ideal gift, and that even if the bride receives two or three such scarves, she will easily be able to find a good use for them.

It is not within everybody's means, of course, to purchase long scarves of fine real lace, but excellent imitation laces can be procured nowadays, especially in Limerick and Mechlin patterns, which are almost as effective as the real thing, and easily within reach of the most modest purse. Our sketches give some picturesque suggestions for the arrangement of a Mechlin lace scarf measuring about two and a half yards in length by

fifteen or sixteen inches in width. No matter how the scarf is arranged, the lace itself will be left intact, and will not need to be cut or damaged in the slightest degree.

As a Fichu

One of the most becoming ways in which to wear a long lace scarf is to drape it lightly round the shoulders, and to allow the long ends to fall on to the front of the skirt. The folds give width to the shoulders, and make the waist appear small by contrast ; while the cascaded draperies, coming to a fine point, give length and elegance to the figure. The black velvet bow which holds the folds together at the waist lends a touch of distinction to the fichu.

In the case of youthful wearers, a single rose might be substituted for this velvet bow, and the folds of the fichu might be caught together higher or lower to suit the figure of the wearer. It is a pretty idea, too, to catch up the lace with a velvet bow in the centre of the back, thus giving that cape effect that is always becoming.

As a Shoulder Scarf

The figure, of which a back view is given, shows a simple but graceful way in which a lace scarf may be used to give a finishing touch to a simple evening gown. Considerable care is needed to drape the folds lightly but securely round the shoulders, and it is a good plan to fasten the scarf to the bodice on one side with quite a small brooch or jewelled pin, so that there shall be no risk of losing it in a crowded room ; but this must be arranged very carefully, or it may tear the lace.

As a variation of this arrangement the scarf may be folded in two, lengthwise, and the folds caught together with a few firm stitches at a distance of about half a yard from the end. When the scarf is draped round the shoulders, this will give a burnous effect, with a pointed hood of lace. The point might be weighted with a gold or silver tassel, which can easily be removed when the wearer wishes to arrange her scarf in a different way.

As a Hood

A lace scarf makes an ideal evening hood, as it gives a surprising amount of warmth, and its

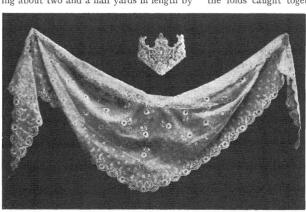

Old English lace scarf of early 19th century work. The Brussels ornament above the scarf is intended to serve as an end for narrow muslin scarf

43

light weight will not damage the most
elaborate coiffure. A sketch is given of a
very becoming hood of this kind, which can
be quite simply arranged by folding the scarf
in the centre, and then using it with the double
lace, draping it once round the head and securing
it at the side with a safety hook and eye.
This fastening is entirely hidden by a cluster
of roses, a picturesque touch which adds greatly
to the charm of the hood. Other flowers might
be substituted to suit the rest of the toilette, or
a bow of velvet or ribbon might be used instead.

As a Mantilla

A more fanciful arrangement of a scarf in
the shape of a mantilla is the subject of

The scarf used as
an evening hood.
Such a wrap will not
disarrange an elaborate
coiffure

A Mechlin lace scarf worn as a fichu. This is a most becoming style
in which to wear a scarf

our last remarks, and for a drapery of this
kind, Spanish lace, either white or black, is
most appropriate. The folds of lace are
doubled in this case also, and draped round the
head, where they must be lightly pinned to the
hair behind a tall Spanish comb of dark
tortoiseshell. The long lace ends are then
brought across the front of the bodice and
taken lightly over the shoulder, so that they
fall gracefully on to the back of the skirt.

This way of wearing a scarf is becoming to
every age and figure, but perhaps more
particularly is it suited to the tall, graceful
brunette, on whom it looks peculiarly "at
home." The hair, of course, should be carefully
dressed in order that the comb may be in the
correct position for the mantilla to hang in
graceful folds, or the effect is lost.

The following are good firms for supplying materials, etc, mentioned in
this Section : Messrs. Clark & Co. (Dyeing and Cleaning) ; Grenfell, Frazier
& Co. (Jewellery) ; Horrockses' (Longcloths and Sheetings, Wholesale only) ;
London Glove Co. (Gloves) ; J. H. B. Dawson, Ltd. (Stork Baby Pants).

The lace worn as a shoulder scarf. This mode lends a
charming finishing touch to an evening gown

44

WOMAN'S DRESS

Conducted by the Editress of "Fashions for All"

In this important section of EVERY WOMAN'S ENCYCLOPÆDIA every aspect of dress will be dealt with by practical and experienced writers. The history of dress from earliest times will be told, and practical and useful information will be given in :

Home Dressmaking		Millinery
How to Cut Patterns	*Home Tailoring*	*Lessons in Hat Trimming*
Methods of Self-measure-	*Representative Fashions*	*How to Make a Shape*
ment	*Fancy Dress*	*How to Curl Feathers*
Colour Contrasts	*Alteration of Clothes, etc.*	*Flowers, Hat-pins, Colours, etc.*
Boots and Shoes	**Furs**	**Gloves**
Choice	*Choice*	*Choice*
How to Keep in Good Condition	*How to Preserve, etc.*	*Cleaning, etc.*
How to Soften Leather, etc.	*How to Detect Frauds*	**Jewellery, etc.**

PRACTICAL ADVICE ON THE CHOICE OF FURS

By THE HON. MRS. FITZROY STEWART

Continued from page 519, Part 4

No. 5. CHINCHILLA, SEA-OTTER, AND OTHER FURS

CHINCHILLA ranks among the six precious furs, and, at the present moment, has reached a price which may be called prohibitive.

The chinchilla is a small rodent of the squirrel species, and comes from South America. It is found chiefly in Peru and Chili, and has its home far up in the Andes. The best skins are imported from Buenos Ayres and Valparaiso.

Chinchilla fur is exquisite in texture, and delicate beyond expression. It is fine and soft to the touch, and of a clear, bluish grey colour above, passing almost into white on the under parts of the body. Skins such as these come from the pure-bred chinchilla, and the cheaper sort from the cross-bred animal. Chinchilla fur shows a strange mixture of qualities.

Cost of Furs

Furriers classify the fur as follows : The best skins come from Peru, the next quality from La Plata, and the third and poorest from Bolivia. The finest Peru skins cost from £20 to £25 a piece ; those from La Plata about £15 ; and skins from Bolivia are worth from £8 to £12. The high price which the finest chinchilla has attained may be seen from the following figures. A long, wide stole and a big muff of Peru

skins recently made to order were priced at no less a sum than £2,000. This triumph of the furrier's art came from one of the best shops in London. A three-quarter length coat of the same fur would cost over £1,000, and a muff might run from £500 to £650. A coat of La Plata fur could be secured from £350 to £500. But skins of fair quality can be procured at a more reasonable rate. I who write have seen a good chinchilla muff at £50 and a stole from £60 to £80.

The Chinchilla

Chinchilla, also, is a costly fur on account of its bad-wearing qualities. The colour soon fades, and a London winter means ruin to our cherished chinchilla. Then the skins are thin and tender, and need the most careful manipulation. In fact, the high price of chinchilla, its fragile nature, and the small size of the skins make it one of the most expensive furs in existence.

The chinchilla in form and character approaches nearly to the hare and rabbit. Its body is from nine to twelve inches in length, and its tail is usually six inches. It has big, soft, black eyes, large roundish ears, a bushy tail, long hind-legs, and long moustaches. It is subterranean in its habits. lives chiefly in holes among the rocks, and climbs and jumps with great agility. Like most wild things, it is hard to catch, and each year seems to go further away into its rocky fastnesses and to become more unattainable. Also demand regulates supply, and there are those who fear that the chinchilla may be fated to become extinct in a not distant future.

The Fraudulent Imitation

But, sad to say, chinchilla fur lends itself easily to base imitations.

This can be done by means of white rabbit dyed grey, or by clipping and tinting white hare. But, in either case, the result is a poor substitute, and, even to an unpractised eye, more or less easy of detection.

In a previous article mention was made of the recent action of the London Chamber of Commerce in warning the public through the Press of the misnaming of furs and their incorrect description. In a list in my possession the proper name for sham chinchilla is stated to be " White rabbit (dyed) " ; the incorrect term, " Chinchilla " ; and the permissible style, " Chinchilla coney." But these authorised names too often lend themselves to trickery. However, in a good shop, one relies on the word of one's furrier.

Chinchilla seems to have been a fur that was not much known to the ancients ; but in the early history of Peru mention is made of the way in which it was used by the Incas. They wove the hair into a sort of cloth, and the skins, with their dainty fur, made a rich lining for the mantles of their chiefs and nobles. And it is curious to note that the great painters of olden days failed to immortalise chinchilla. Their sitters were decked with sable and ermine, but the soft, grey fur had few admirers.

Chinchilla ranks with silver fox as a fur that is always harmonious. And, on this account, it stands high in favour with the best-dressed women in London, Paris, and Vienna. But chinchilla looks its best when worn by a decided brunette, or, at any rate, by a wearer who has a perfect complexion. It is a fur which needs definite tints, dark hair for choice, or else golden or auburn hair, and, in either case, much brilliance of colouring. For the grey tones of chinchilla accentuate the dull shades of a bad complexion, and it should never be worn by a woman whose skin has the least hint of sallowness. Some women spend large sums on a chinchilla coat or stole—grey, colourless women, who make a sad mistake when they match their clothes to their complexions.

Colours to Wear with Chinchilla

Then this grey fur must be carefully matched with one's other garments. Chinchilla, on no account, should be worn with a brown or fawn frock, but looks its best with grey or black or with a dull shade of mauve or violet. Like sable, it resents bright colours and crude combinations. And it does not trim well, but makes a splendid collar and cuffs to a coat or cloak of black velvet. Then, like ermine and silver fox, it should always be worn with rich materials. It suits neither sport nor travel, nor the simple life, nor any sort of rough surroundings.

Parisians class it with ermine as a fur for spring and early autumn. Indeed, in our recent chilly summers, a chinchilla stole and muff worn with a grey chiffon gown looked—and felt—to great advantage

Sable, sealskin, silver fox, ermine, and chinchilla make five precious furs, and the sixth is represented by sea-otter. This latter is the imperial fur of China, and is at once one of the most costly and durable of furs in existence. Sea-otter is rarely seen except as the collar of a man's coat or of a long fur coat for a woman. One skin suffices for a collar, facing, and cuffs, and in the best quality would cost from £350 to £500.

The sea-otter has its home in the North Pacific, near the Aleutian Islands, and is a powerful creature, often four feet long and ninety pounds in weight, with a strong jaw and massive molars. Its fur is dense, rich, rather long, very fine, and of a dark-brown colour ; and silver hairs are found in some of the best specimens. Sea-otter as a fur has one great advantage, it is rarely or never imitated. It is highly prized in Russia, and much worn by men of the Russian nobility.

Opossum as a Substitute

Since the world began and fig-leaves went out of fashion, no woman has ever had money enough to dress upon, and this whether her allowance is £100 a year or £1,000.

But the wind is tempered to the shorn lamb, and the would-be economist can and will escape from her difficulties. For instance, opossum makes a by no means bad substitute for chinchilla. This fur has two varieties. The best is soft to the touch, of a delicate bluish-grey colour, and comes from Australia. And another animal of the same species has rather hard, wiry fur of a brownish shade, and is found in Virginia and other parts of North America. The skins are small, and their price varies from three shillings to £1 a piece and upwards.

Opossum fur looks best in stoles and for muffs and neckties. It is unsuitable for coats on account of its thickness and fluffiness. Articles made of this fur are moderate in price ; a stole of the best grey opossum would cost from £20 to £25, and a muff might be about £10. Opossum has for some time past been a favourite fur in Paris, but has never caught on in London and England. In fact, as regards fashion in fur we seem to be strictly conservative. A year or two ago there was a run on fisher fur in Paris, and now they are using *puteau*, the dark, silky skin of a sort of rat, and neither of these have as yet found much favour in London. As a nation, we are faithful to sable, ermine, sealskin, several sorts of foxes, chinchilla, and now and then to sea-otter.

With regard to these two latter, those in the know declare that the animals have of late become much rarer, and that measures must be taken to prevent their extermination. And as to sable, silver fox, and ermine, there can be no doubt but that year by year the crop gets steadily smaller. And this can be easily explained if we think of their natural habits. The creatures which yield the better sorts of fur are exceedingly wild, and as the half-savage trappers who capture them prosecute their search into more distant parts, the animals flee further north or higher into the mountains, and find it more difficult to procure food in these remote regions.

Buying Furs

From time to time ideas have been started as to the possibility of retaining the more valuable fur-bearing creatures within a fenced enclosure. And some years ago a fantastic scheme to harbour and foster the sable in its own home was seriously attempted. But the experiment proved a failure. The sables lost their health, and the skins were poor—yellow in hue and coarse and brittle in texture. Fine close fur is found only upon animals which live in conditions of the greatest hardship and range over a vast territory. Most of us wear furs, but not one woman in a hundred knows much on the subject. There are three things the choice of which needs the knowledge of an expert ; and these three are furs, jewels, and old furniture. And the two first seem the most difficult of selection, for they affect one's looks, and we all of us know that in the world of to-day a

A beautiful chinchilla coat and muff. Chinchilla is one of the most costly and fragile of furs, and is best suited to a brunette with a good complexion

Reutlinger

woman's best asset is her charm of appearance. And in this respect furs go one better than jewels, for they form at once a frame and a background.

Now for a word on the science of shopping. First money is wanted, then brains, good taste, and some experience. No one should be taken in by so-called bargains in any of the finer skins, for there will never be a glut in the market of sable, silver fox, sealskin, ermine, or chinchilla. But a reduction in price may be got by ready-money payments.

Then, if economy must be studied, I would advise a woman to buy good and hardwearing furs rather than the fragile sort or those which are but the fancy of the moment. Then she must also take thought of her personal appearance. Furs divide themselves into neutral, brown, black, and white, and can be classified according to texture into flat, fluffy, and velvety. A stout woman will look her best in the smooth velvety furs that are of a dark shade, such as sealskin or musquash, and should carefully avoid fluffy, long-haired skins, such as skunk, bear, and opossum. Sable and sealskin and silver fox suit most of us, while chinchilla favours brunettes, but both it and ermine demand good complexions.

Variety Needed

Then the *mondaine* of to-day wants several sets of furs. Her Russian sables will not content her with all her frocks, although they are beautiful with many. She will need chinchilla with her grey gowns, and will want silver fox to wear with brighter colours, and sealskin and moleskin for the country and travelling. And certain furs seem to do best in the evening. These include ermine as a cloak or stole, and white fox or white Thibet goat as a trimming for a cloak or wrapper.

This series will be continued.

PRACTICAL LESSONS IN DRESSMAKING

Continued from page 523, Part 4

By M. PRINCE BROWNE

Examiner in Dressmaking, Tailoring, French Pattern Modelling, Plain Needlework, and Millinery, of the Teachers in Training at the University College of South Wales and Monmouthshire, Cardiff; the London Higher Technical Examination Centres, etc. ; First Class Diploma for Tailoring ; Diploma of Honour for Dressmaking ; Diploma of Merit of the Highest Order for Teaching ; Silver Medallist, London Exhibition, 1900 ; Silver Medal, Franco-British Exhibition, 1908 ; Author of " Up-to-Date Dresscutting and Drafting," also " The Practical Work of Dressmaking and Tailoring."

FIFTH LESSON. A SIMPLE SKIRT

A Simple Walking Skirt—How to Measure for a Skirt—Drafting the Gores—Fitting the Skirt

THIS skirt can be made of serge, tweed, etc. Three and a quarter yards of material, 54 inches wide, would be required for a skirt 42 inches in length. The measurements of the person for whom it is to be made must be ascertained. Take the waist measure first, rather tight ; then round the hips, about 7 inches below the waist, rather loose. Measure the length of the front, from the *bottom* of the waistband to the *floor* ; the side, from the bottom of the waistband over the fullest part of the hips to the floor, on the *right* and *left* side.

N.B.—The size of the hips is not always the same on both sides, and where this is the case allowance must be made for it, or the skirt will not hang perfectly even all round. Next measure the back, from the bottom of the waistband to the floor.

The person must stand *perfectly erect* while these measurements are being taken, and they must all be to the floor, but the skirt can be made any length desired. For a useful walking skirt, it should be the same distance off the ground all round, about two or more inches, but this is a matter of fashion.

The measurements taken in this way should be kept, as any style of skirt can be made from them.

Whatever material is used for an unlined skirt should be of a *good* and *firm* make. Black or navy Estamene serge (shrunk), 54 inches wide, can be had from 3s. 3d. per yard, and cream serge (shrunk) for 3s. 4d. There is no up and down to a serge, so the gores may be cut some one way and some the other (if it will economise the cloth); but, of course, all the gores must be cut selvedgewise and not across the material.

As there is a right and wrong side to serge, care must be taken that the gores of one side of the skirt " face " the other, and that they are not all cut for the one side.

To ascertain the right side of serge, place it on the table, look at it from the *cut* edge, and if the diagonal lines run from *left* to *right*, it is the right side; if from *right* to *left*, it is the wrong side. If the gores can be cut from the serge folded double, they will, of course, match. Three and a quarter yards of material, 54 inches wide, are required for a skirt 24 inches round the waist, 42 inches round the hips, and 42 inches in length all round.

Open out the material, and place it *wrong* side uppermost on the table, and, with a

piece of tailor's chalk and two tailor's squares (see Lesson on Tailoring in Part 1), draft the skirt on the material from the measurements (no pattern is necessary).

From the " cut edge " measure down the selvedge 4½ inches (for the hem and turning), and make a mark. From it, measure 42½ inches (the length the skirt is to be when

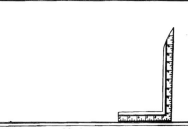

Diagram I. Squaring the rule

finished, plus half an inch for turning at the waist) and make a mark, and three inches beyond it, make another mark. At *this point* square the rule (as shown in Diagram 1) by the selvedge, and draw a line 12 inches long (half the waist measure) and a curved line for the waist from the mark on the selvedge to the end of the line just made (as shown on Diagram 2).

Draw to the left a second curved line, 7 inches below the curve for the waist, for the hip measure. Deduct 3 inches from the half *hip* measure (21 inches), and measure along the hip line 18 inches, and make a mark.

Place two squares with the short arms side by side as illustrated in the first Lesson on Tailoring in Part 1), and the long arms forming one long line from the *end* of the " curve for waist," passing *through* the mark on the hip line, and draw a long dotted line for the centre-back seam. From it, measure 1½ inches, and draw a long chalk line for the turning.

N.B.—This extra wide turning on the back seam is an advantage, as it makes the skirt hang better.

From the " curve for waist," measure down the centre-back seam 42½ inches (the length for the back of the skirt, plus

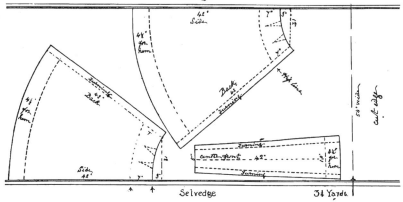

Diagram 2.   Drafting the skirt

half an inch for turnings), and make a mark. Take a tape measure, and hold the end of it with the thumb and forefinger of the left hand *on* " the curve for waist " where it touches the selvedge. Take a piece of tailor's chalk in the right hand, hold it *upright* in the tape measure, *exactly on* the mark denoting the length of the skirt and turning (42½ inches), and mark round with the chalk for the bottom of the skirt from the selvedge to the centre-back line, moving the two hands simultaneously—the *left* one more slowly along the " curve for waist." The tape measure must be *tightly* extended between the two hands *all* the time the dotted line is being drawn. Still holding the *left* hand in the same position, place the chalk 4½ inches lower down the tape measure, and draw a second line for the hem and turning. Cut the material out *on* the chalk lines all round (*none* of the dotted lines must be cut), and place the piece along the opposite selvedge of the material, in the position shown on the diagram, with the wrong side facing the wrong side of the material, and cut out the second piece *exactly* the same size as the first. For this skirt the front should be 5 inches wide at the top and 10 inches at the bottom, plus 1 inch on *each* side for the turnings. To draft it, measure from the selvedge *across* the material 4 inches, and make a mark ; from it, measure down 42½ inches (for the length of skirt when finished, plus half an inch for turning at the waist), make a mark, and with the squares draw a dotted line *parallel* to the selvedge from one mark to the other ; this gives the centre of the front. Measure and mark 2½ inches on each side of the dotted line, and for the bottom, measure and mark 5 inches on each side of the other end of the dotted line, and with the squares draw a slanting, dotted line from one mark to the other on each side. From each of these slanting lines measure and mark 1 inch for turnings, and draw two long chalk

lines. Draw a chalk line across the top and a dotted line across the bottom. Beyond this dotted line measure 4½ inches for the hem and turning, and draw a chalk line across as shown in the diagram. Cut out the front *on* the chalk lines. The three pieces of the skirt are now ready to be put together. Place one of the gores, *right* side uppermost, flat on the table, and lay the front, *wrong* side uppermost, over it, with the edge level with the straight side of the gore, and the *top* edges of the two pieces quite even. Pin, and then tack them together all down the dotted line on the side of the front. Place the second gore, right side uppermost, on the table, and lay the other side of the front, wrong side uppermost, over it, with the edge level with the straight side of the gore, and the top edges of the two pieces quite even. Pin, and then tack them together down the dotted line on the side of the front.

N.B.—The seams of every skirt must be pinned, and then tacked, from the top downwards, and this must always be done flat on the table, or the seams will be puckered.

The straight of each gore must *always* be placed towards the front, or if the gores are sloped on both sides, the side which is *least* sloped must be placed towards the front.

The home-worker will find it easier to fit the skirt before the back seam is joined, and it should *always* be fitted right side out. Pin the skirt at the centre of the front to the figure or dress-stand, bring the skirt round smoothly, but not strained, over the hips (about 7 inches below the waist), pin it together at the back, and again pin it to the figure or stand at the waist.

The top of this skirt must be reduced to the size of the waist by means of two darts on each side. The space between the two darts should be the same as that between the side-seam and the first dart.

To be continued.

49

DRESS IN THE STUART PERIOD

A SOURCE OF INSPIRATION TO MODERN DESIGNERS

By MARY HOWARTH

Continued from page 385, Part 3.

Dress in the Age of Louis XIV.—The Effect of the Restoration upon Costume

To avoid recognition, black velvet masks lined with white satin were worn at this period. They folded in two like a man's pocket-book and so were very easily carried. Neither were there any strings with which to have to fumble when the moment for masking arrived. Instead of them a slender silver bar was provided on the inside of the mask, ending in a button which the wearer of the mask placed between her teeth so that she could hold her face-screen in its place. Women wore masks during the public promenade, at balls, and even in church. There were different patterns. Some hid the eyes only, others covered the face more completely and were a thorough disguise, not only because they obliterated the features but because, worn over the mouth, they changed the " timbre " of the voice.

In France during the minority of Louis XIV., when political troubles were rife and the great ladies of the day played their part in them, masks were used for a more serious purpose. Conspiracies were cradled in the boudoirs of the wealthy, and those great dames to whom the name of "belles frondeuses " was given, in allusion to the troubles of the Fronde, went masked to the councils of Condé and Beaufort in order to escape observation.

To pass to a more frivolous subject, let that of jewellery now take precedence. It was owing to the influence of Charles II. and his early life in France that the women of the Restoration Court were more wonderfully dressed and gorgeously bedizened than any who had been before. The reaction after the sober guise of the Commonwealth accounted for exaggerations of all kinds, and extravagance in every direction reigned supreme. The materials worn were absolutely superb, and into them were woven silver and gold, while they were thickly plastered with jewels for high days and holidays.

Bodices were laced with pearls, festooned with diamonds, throats encircled with ropes of pearls, exquisite brooches and galaxies of jewels decked the corsage, the sleeves, and the hair of the great ladies of the day.

Jewellers of our own times keep ever before them ornaments worn in the reign of the Merry Monarch, and now, as then, ropes of pearls, rivulets of diamonds and emeralds,

and the great round boss brooches fringed with gems are fashionable.

When the hair was not decorated with a string of pearls a ribbon ornament was substituted, another source of inspiration for the coiffure decorations of our own day. Women wore their hair curled, and arranged with the greatest skill, adding to it in many instances what were called " heart-breakers," artificial ringlets posed at the side of the head on a neat arrangement of wires.

In the latter part of the reign of Charles II. hoods came into fashion, and were issued in various patterns, all of them bewitchingly quaint and charming. It was customary then to paint the face as well as to patch it, an act of vanity that was criticised with the greatest severity by Richard Baxter and other purists.

" I am no judge of painting," replied a Turkish Ambassador who was interrogated as to his opinion of the beauty of Frenchwomen.

There is a chronicle of the dresses worn at the festivities of a Royal betrothal in France which gives so graphic an idea of the apparel of the time that it is well worth repetition. The Duchesse de Bourgogne wore one day a gown of silver tissue with gold flowers, touched with a little flame colour and green, and in her hair the finest of the Crown diamonds. Her gown on the next day was of grey damask with silver flowers, and her jewels were diamonds and emeralds.

Mademoiselle (the young fiancée) wore a coat of *gros de Tours* richly embroidered in gold, and a skirt of silver tissue embroidered in gold touched with flame colour. She was adorned by a splendid set of diamonds and a mantle of gold *point d'Espagne*, six yards and a half long—two and a half more than the Court trains of to-day. On another occasion her coat and skirt were both made of cloth of silver, and her jewels were diamonds and rubies.

The famous Madame de Maintenon introduced to the jewel-casket the cross called à la Maintenon. At that time she set a fashion for severity in attire, which consisted of forbidding-looking coifs and veils and black and sombre dresses.

The inauguration of fashions by the great Court ladies and the Parisian actresses of the period was a feature of the times. It happened one day that the beautiful Duchesse de Fontanges was present at a Royal hunting party, when a breeze disarranged her head-dress. Promptly she tied it in its place by means of her ribbon garters, the ends of which fell over her forehead. Louis XIV. was so fascinated by this improvised novel effect that a head-dress, called à la Fontange, was instantly adopted by the ladies of the Court and afterwards by the Parisian bourgeoises.

It was a framework of cap wire about half a yard in height, divided into tiers and positively covered with bands of muslin, ribbons, flowers, chenille, and up-standing aigrettes. To each tier of the structure names were given such as the Duke, the Duchess, the Capuchin, the Solitary One, the Asparagus, the Cabbage, the Cat, the Organ Pipe, the First or Second Sky and the Mouse. The last a little bow of "nonpareil" fixed in the fringe of crisply waving hair that was arranged below the curled "fontange."

The fashionable woman of these days was as inseparable from her pet dog as is her descendant of to-day. She therefore carried it in her muff, which was large and flat, and as limp as quite recently fashionable muffs have been. The dogs were small and went by the name of muff-dogs.

It was a thoughtless age. How the " French kickshaws " of the Court must have annoyed the sense of decorum cherished by the Puritans, who " shook their heads at folks in London." But it was a picturesque one, too. The Roundheads, for all they were as simply clad as could be, left us a heritage of the prettiest and most demure of fashions. We should not have known

Mary Queen of Scots
Portrait similar to the one at Hampton Court by Mytens

the full skirt hanging straight and un-adorned, the big white apron and the hood, so closely tied beneath the chin that scarcely a wisp of hair was revealed, prettiest of frames for the sweet, unpainted face if the Puritans had not designed them for us. The pure white muslin " tippit " and the sensible square-toed shoes—would any mind save that spurred to a sense of violent contrast by the extreme modes of an opposing faction have thought of aught so seriously sweet ? To the riot of bright hues the Royalists approved, to the musk-coloured silks and the starches of various tints they brought and used as a sedative; cold greys and duns and blacks they deemed suitable for the clothing of their poor flesh.

The renowned diarist Pepys gives us a vivid picture of the great ladies in their fine array, interspersed with references to his own fine " camlet " and " jackanapes " coats and his wife's " new yellow bird's-eye hood " and other delicate pieces of apparel.

It is not amazing that the children's dress of that day serves as a copy for those of small damsels and boys who are to act as attendants and pages in wedding retinues to-day. They were garbed then in replicas of the picturesque grown-up attire, the little maids with stiff satin frocks falling to the floor and the little boys in satin knickerbockers and coats and silken hose with rosetted shoes. Their hair was cut across the forehead in a fringe and fell softly about their broad lace collars.

The painters of the period, such as Sir Peter Lely and Van Dyck, indeed, afford an endless source of inspiration to the designers of modern dress.

PRACTICAL LESSONS IN TAILORING

FOR HOME WORKERS AND OTHERS

By M. PRINCE BROWNE

Examiner in Dressmaking, Tailoring, French Pattern Modelling, Millinery, and Plain Needlework of the Teachers in Training at the University College of South Wales and Monmouthshire, Cardiff, the London Technical Examination Centre, etc. Author of " Up-to-Date Dresscutting and Drafting," also " The Practical Work of Dressmaking and Tailoring,"

Continued from page 525, Part 4

FIFTH LESSON. POCKETS—*continued*

Circular Pockets (continued)—Roll Collar—Revers—Padding

To make the pocket, cut two pieces of lining rather wider than the opening and the depth the pocket is to be, and face the top of one piece on the right side (about three inches down) with a piece of the cloth ; this is to prevent the lining showing through the opening.

N.B.—If a circular pocket is being made in a coat, the lining must, of course, match that of the coat.

Place the piece of lining which has been faced, wrong side uppermost, on the wrong side of the cloth, with the facing over the opening, the facing to be towards the top of the opening ; tack it in this position along the top (as near as possible to the curved line) to the piece of linen, and machine-stitch it to this, but *not* through to the cloth representing the coat.

Take the second piece of lining which is to form the pocket, and place it *wrong* side uppermost, with the edge to the *lower* edge of the linen, and the pocket piece facing upwards. Tack and stitch this to the *lower* edge of the linen, and as near as possible to the curved line ; but do not stitch through to the cloth.

Turn *both* pieces for the pocket *downwards*, and stitch them together all round, but no stitches must be taken through to the piece of cloth, representing the coat, in which the pocket is being made.

Take a small piece of linen and hold it under one corner, on the wrong side of the pocket, and fix it firmly in this position by " private stitching " it through from the right side of the piece of cloth (or coat), *prodding* the needle up and down several times. Do the other corner of the pocket with a small piece of linen in the same way.

These small pieces of linen are stitched under the corners to strengthen them, and to prevent the pocket stretching out of shape with use. From the *right* side of the piece of cloth (or coat) " private stitch " round the top curve of the opening *right through to the pocket.* If this is not done a " flap " will be found at the top of the curve when the tacking (illustrated in diagram No. 4, Part 4), which keeps the two edges of the opening together, is removed. In making a coat it is better to leave the opening of the pocket tacked across until the coat is quite finished.

N.B.—Private stitching is always done by

hand, with some of the same kind of silk with which the machine-stitching has been done, and *each* stitch must be worked *over* a machine-stitch, so that it may appear *one with it* and not show ; it is because it must be invisible that it is called " private stitching."

It is used to fix the corners of pockets, or any part · which has been previously stitched (for ornament), but requires to be fastened down securely and invisibly.

Roll Collar and Revers ·

A " roll collar " is cut, worked, pressed, and then put on to the coat and " faced " ; the " revers " are cut *in one* with the fronts of the coat, but as the worker has not yet learned to make a coat, the collar and revers (like the pockets) can be made for practice on a piece of cloth.

A good guide for the length of the collar is the size of the neck (measured round the base) plus one inch—*e.g.*, if the neck measure is 14 inches, the collar should be 15 inches long, and 3 or 3½ inches deep. Take a piece of French canvas, and measure about eleven inches along the selvedge, and make a mark, and about 11 inches along the cut edge make another mark. Place a tailor's square across the corner of the canvas from one

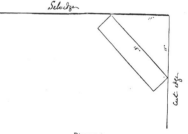

Selvedge

Cut edge

Diagram 1

mark to the other, and draw a line with a pencil or piece of French chalk ; on this line measure and mark the 15 inches (for the length of the collar), and from each end of the line measure and mark 3 or 3½ inches for the depth of the collar. Place the square from one mark to the other, and draw a second line parallel to the first and 15 inches long, and connect these two lines by two short perpendicular lines (as in diagram No. 1).

This gives the net size the collar is to be when finished.

The canvas must always be cut *exactly* to the measurements ; no turnings are needed or must be allowed.

N.B.—If the collar is being cut from a small piece of canvas from which the selvedge has been removed, great care must be taken to cut the collar *perfectly* on the cross, or it will not set.

If a sufficiently large piece of canvas is not available, several pieces can be joined

Diagram 2. Herringbone down the raw edges

together, provided the *joins* are all made on the straight ; the raw edges are placed one over the other and herringboned down, as shown in diagram No. 2.

Instructions for herringboning were given in the Dressmaking lesson in Part 3, but in joining the pieces of canvas together the stitches must be taken through the two folds to secure them firmly together.

Cut out the crossway piece *exactly on* the lines, make a mark at the edge of the canvas at half its length, from this mark measure 1 inch or more, *up*, and make another mark ; this gives the depth for the " stand " of the collar.

Measure from each end 2 inches or less, make a mark, and draw a curved line from it to the mark, which is 1 inch (or more) *up*, at the centre. Fold the canvas in half—with the curved line outside—and trace through it to the under half with a tracing-wheel ; this ensures the two halves being exactly alike. Cut a small piece off the canvas at the ends (from the mark at 2 inches from the end), taking off about a quarter of an inch of the depth of the collar, unfold the canvas, and draw over the traced line to perfect the curve. The canvas is now ready to be put on to the cloth ; the underside of the collar must be done first.

Place a piece of cloth to match the coat (when a coat is being made) wrong side uppermost on the table, and put the piece of canvas (with the curved line uppermost) along, and about half an inch from, the cut edge of the cloth ; tack them together loosely along the centre with three or four stitches only.

N.B.—If the cloth is " faced," the canvas must be tacked to it so that the " face " will smooth downwards.

Cut out the cloth, leaving about half an inch all round beyond the canvas for turning.

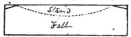

Diagram 3. Run neatly round the curved line

Thread a needle with silk to match the cloth in colour, make a knot, and, holding the canvas uppermost, *run neatly* round the curved line, taking *only* one stitch at a time, draw the row of running rather tight, and fasten it off firmly at the end

(see diagram No. 3). This row of running stitches divides the " stand " from the " fall " of the collar, and the tightness prevents the back of the collar stretching and standing out from the neck of the wearer.

The Collar must now be Padded

Padding is a stitch used in tailoring to secure canvas to cloth in collars, revers, etc., and to make them " roll " ; also to keep two pieces of canvas together to interline and stiffen fancy collars, revers, cuffs, etc.

To pad the collar commence with the " fall," hold it lengthwise, canvas uppermost, *over* the first finger of the left hand, with the curved row of running stitches to the right. Thread a needle with fine silk to match the cloth, make a knot, and take a short, straight stitch from right to left through the canvas to the cloth, close to the row of running stitches dividing the " stand " from the " fall " ; this will form a small stitch on the cloth side. Make a second short, straight stitch from right to left, about a

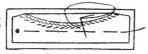

Diagram 4. How to commence the padding

quarter of an inch above the first stitch ; this will form a slanting stitch on the canvas, and another straight stitch on the cloth (see diagram No. 4). Continue working in this way to the end of the curved line of running, then, *without turning* the work, but still holding it in the same position, work *back* again, making each straight stitch start from the middle of the slanting stitch in the last row, but not touching it. Continue to work these stitches backwards and forwards without turning the work at all, until the whole of the " fall " has been padded. Turn the collar round, and pad the " stand " in the same way, backwards and forwards *from the row of trimming* and lengthwise of the collar, holding the " fall " to the right, and working as before until the whole of the " stand " has been padded (see diagram No. 5.)

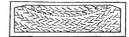

Diagram 5. How the padding should look when finished

N.B.—Great care must be taken when padding to *hold the work correctly*, or the shape of the collar or revers will be spoiled. The work must be held *over* the finger the *whole* time, *lengthwise* of the collar or revers, thus allowing the canvas to become longer than the cloth which is underneath, and making the collar or revers " roll."

The edges of the cloth must next be turned down over the canvas, and neatly tacked near the edge all round. All superfluous cloth must be cut away at the corners, so that they may lie perfectly flat.

To be continued.

The following are good firms for supplying materials, etc., mentioned in this Section : Messrs. Clark & Co. (Dyeing and Cleaning) ; Horrockses (Longcloths and Sheetings—Wholesale only).

WOMAN'S DRESS
Conducted by the Editress of "Fashions For All"

In this important section of EVERY WOMAN'S ENCYCLOPÆDIA every aspect of dress will be dealt with by practical and experienced writers. The history of dress from earliest times will be told, and practical and useful information will be given in :

Home Dressmaking		Millinery
How to Cut Patterns	*Home Tailoring*	*Lessons in Hat Trimming*
Methods of Self-measure-	*Representative Fashions*	*How to Make a Shape*
ment	*Fancy Dress*	*How to Curl Feathers*
Colour Contrasts	*Alteration of Clothes, etc.*	*Flowers, Hat-pins, Colours, etc.*
Boots and Shoes	**Furs**	**Gloves**
Choice	*Choice*	*Choice*
How to Keep in Good Condition	*How to Preserve, etc.*	*Cleaning, etc.*
How to Soften Leather, etc.	*How to Detect Frauds*	**Jewellery, etc.**

PRACTICAL ADVICE ON THE CHOICE OF FURS

By THE HON. MRS. FITZROY STEWART

Continued from page 636, Part 5

No. 6. LESS EXPENSIVE FURS

Some Furs that are within the reach of Women with Moderate Incomes—Bear, Beaver, Persian Lamb, Broadtail, Skunk, Moleskin, Mink

THE purse of Fortunatus is a pleasant possession but a rare one, and most of us suffer from a decided shortage of cash.

One's sympathies are with the average woman, who has her place in the world, a pretty face, a taste for luxury, and a dismal lack of the one thing needful. Previous articles have shown that to acquire the six precious furs costs hundreds of pounds. But the poorer woman has at her hand some useful substitutes, such as bear, beaver, crimmer, fisher, goat, genet, mink, marten, moleskin, musquash, nutria, Persian lamb, skunk, squirrel, and wolverine.

Bear Fur

Bear fur is most becoming. Soft, dark fur adds to a woman's beauty, and there is in a certain type of face, handsome and hard-featured, that looks its best when softened by what may be termed a ragged fur, such as the best brown bear, skunk, or even goat, whether known as Thibet or Mongolian.

Bear fur is in three different colours, brown, black, and white. The brown bear inhabits Russia, the Caucasus, part of Norway, and Upper Hungary. Its fur is thick, long, and glossy, heavy in weight, but of immense durability. ·Cub skins are highly prized on account of their softness and fine texture, but their small size makes the skins more expensive. A good bear skin costs £10, and one of the best quality might be £15. A stole of the best fur is worth about £16, and a muff about £7. But at one furrier's I saw a big muff, like a soft, black pillow, made of two cub skins of great beauty. This muff was priced at £12.

Types of Bear and Beaver

If the fur were not of such good quality, a small stole might be £5 and a muff £3. Brown bear varies in colour from almost black to fawn and cinnamon. The lighter shade of cinnamon, known as Isabella bear, is expensive, but seems now out of favour. A good skin costs £15, and one of these, mounted on fawn cloth, makes a handsome carriage rug, worth about £18.

Black bears come from Canada, and quite 25,000 skins are annually supplied by British North America. They are nearly black in their natural state, but are dyed to make the colour more uniform. This fur is also thick and glossy, but has a certain harshness. A good many skins are bought for military purposes, and are used for the headgear of Guardsmen in the British Army. Black bears are large in size, so one skin makes two caps, and a good skin costs from £14 to £16. Hence the familiar busby is worth about £8.

Bear fur is also used for the collars and linings of the Russian " shubes," or sledge-coats. Coachmen's capes are now out-of-date, but these used to be made from the common and coarser bearskins. The white Polar bear is found all over the Arctic regions, but the finest skins come from Greenland. And these retain their whiteness, because, after flaying, the natives drag them through the snow, which prevents the oil from turning them yellow. Some of these bears are 12 feet in length, but their young are no bigger than rabbits.

Beavers were known to the ancients, and in the fourth century the fur of the beaver, or Pontic dog, as it was called, seems to have been in great demand. The beaver has a way of disappearing from countries where it has once flourished. For instance, it used to be found in England, and is now extinct ; but Lord Bute has introduced beavers with a measure of success into the Isle of Rothesay in Scotland. They are now only really at home in Russia, Poland, Siberia, and North America. The best come from Canada ; and it is worthy of note that the Dominion of Canada chose the beaver for its coat-of-arms, and that in old days beaver skins passed as currency in British North America. This rodent is allied to the squirrel, and has a flat tail about ten inches in length. It is about a foot in

Photo   *Reutlinger*
A becoming and artistic use of skunk on a beautiful wrap. Among the less costly furs mentioned in this article, skunk ranks high both for becoming effect and durability

height, and ten inches in length. Beavers, like seals, have acute senses and a high order of intelligence. They seem to be endowed with reasoning power rather than with instinct, and can adapt their actions to varying conditions. Beaver architecture, as well as human, has its history. Beavers can fell trees and dam streams, and a beaver lodge is a marvellous construction. Some of their dams are said to be a thousand years old.

Beaver fur is much lighter in weight than bear, but like bear has immense durability. Its price is rather high, and a long coat of the best beaver would cost from £40 to £80. A large, long stole would be about £25, and a big muff £16. But cheaper goods can be procured, and a small stole and muff might cost £10 or £12.

In old days beaver was much in demand for the making of hats, gloves, purses, and other articles. Chaucer speaks of a beaver hat in 1386, and in the time of Queen Elizabeth these hats became common, and the fashion continued for nearly three centuries. The beaver skins were usually dyed black, and formed the headgear of the upper classes in Great Britain. In fact, in 1638, an Act of Parliament prohibited the use of any other material for hat-making, and this contributed to the diminution of the number of beavers in North America. An encyclopædia, which shall be nameless, says that " there is no longer such a thing as a genuine beaver hat." But this is a mistake, as white beaver hats are still worn by the servants of Lord Lonsdale and Sir Edwin Durning-Lawrence.

Beaver fur has much in its favour, but it is flat and of a dull colour, and perhaps more useful than either smart or becoming. Bear and beaver are like nothing but themselves, and their fur need not fear imitation.

Persian lamb is a fur produced from sheep found in Persia, and the best skins come from Bokhara. Persian sheep are said to be the most ancient breed of sheep in the world, and this fur is far older than is usually imagined. Some miniver robes of the fifteenth century were carefully examined, and they leave no doubt that the dark fur on them is Persian lamb and not ermine tails. The natural colour of the skin is rusty black, but it is dyed a dense black before use, and this is done either in Canada or Germany. The water of English rivers does not seem suitable for the purpose.

Persian Lamb

The wool of the full-grown sheep is coarse and dense, but, unlike its parent, the skin of the Persian lamb is very soft and curly in the extreme. And this curl is artificially preserved by at once wrapping the skin up in a covering to keep it from contact with the air. These skins are not sold in a raw state in England, but are taken once a year to the fair at Nijni Novgorod by the Tartar owners. They are then sold to Leipsic merchants, who are most skilful dyers and cleaners. Indeed, it can be said that Leipsic supplies the whole world with Persian lamb, which is often, but wrongly, known as astrachan.

Persian lamb has high favour in England, and may be well called the fur of utility. It is most durable, and suits the needs of the woman who walks instead of drives, as it does not spoil with rain, and is by no means aggressive. It must not be reckoned cheap, as a good coat of Persian lamb would cost from £50 to £120. The skins cost from about £1 10s. to £3, and upwards. The fur called caracul is a commoner and cheaper variety. It has no curl, and its hair is longer and more fluffy, but it is lighter than Persian lamb—a decided point in its favour. A caracul coat can be bought for £15, and stoles and muffs in proportion. Broadtail—correctly known as breitzschwanz—is one of the finest furs in the world and of a satin-like softness. The skin is thin and fine, and the fur has no curl, but a waved line on its surface, which reminds one of silk moiré. But breitzschwanz has a gruesome history. It is the coat of the young, unborn lamb, and tender-hearted women often avoid this fur, and in any case its present price is almost prohibitive. The skins are tiny, and each skin is worth from £3 to £6. Some years ago a woman had a coat and short skirt of broadtail fur, which was priced at £500, and at the present time such a get-up would cost perhaps £1,000.

Moleskin

Now to return to the cheaper varieties. Moleskin is, to my mind, one of the most charming furs in existence. It has delicate shades of colour, is soft and downy, and most becoming. In fact, it adds more to a woman's looks than do many of its costlier rivals. Also it is light in weight—to a delicate woman no small advantage. The mole is perhaps too plentiful in Great Britain, but, oddly enough, is not found in Ireland, and not often in Scotland, except in the Isle of Mull. Scotch moles, however, supply the best moleskin. This fur has one fault. Like most dainty things, it is by no means durable. But the price is moderate. A long coat of the best moleskin would cost from £30 to £40, a good stole might be £15, and a big muff can be secured for £4. Ermine is the only fur that goes well with moleskin. An ermine tie helps the effect, and an ermine muff completes the costume.

The mole lives near water. It has a plump body, with a velvet-like coat, and soft fur of a greyish brown colour. Its length is about six inches, and its tiny tail only half an inch long, and it owns stout limbs and a pointed muzzle. It has no visible ears, and its eyes are so minute as to be easily over looked. The mole is a voracious creature, has an unquenchable thirst, and what may be termed a "rage of hunger." It eats no vegetables, but preys on mice, small birds, and tiny animals. Its cleverly designed subterranean labyrinths, with their passages and galleries, are a familiar—for the farmer a too familiar—feature in our fields. Part of the mole's object in constructing them is the pursuit of the earthworms, on which he loves to prey.

Mink Fur

The mink is a species of marten that occurs in Canada and in most parts of North America, but the best skins come from York River in the Hudson Bay Territory. It is an amphibious creature, and feeds chiefly on fish, frogs, and mussels. Its body measures from 12 to 18 inches in length, exclusive of the tail, which is long and bushy. Its hair is fine and soft and of a chestnut brown colour, which varies from a pale shade to the dark hue of the finest sable. The skins most in demand are those that are almost black in colour. Mink skins run from £1 to £6 apiece. They are of small size, and a coat of good mink would cost from £180 to £250 according to length and quality. A stole might be about £36, and a big muff from £14 to £20.

Mink ranks with bear and beaver as one of the best wearing furs in existence. In this it comes before either sable or sealskin, and is second only to sea-otter. Mink fur was at one time so much in request that an attempt was made to establish "minkeries" for the purpose of breeding the animal. But as in the case of sable, it was found that the fur of the mink then so deteriorated as to be almost worthless. Mink of a dark shade is sometimes passed off as Russian sable. But this fraud can easily be detected, as the fur is shorter than sable and much more fluffy. Mention will be made of other cheap furs in a future article.

HOME-MADE COIFFURE DECORATIONS

By LILIAN JOY

Three Pretty Head-dresses—A Head-dress for a Young Girl—How to Make Gold and Silver Fuchsias—Gold Metallic Moiré Ribbon—How to Make Cabochons

THE very simplicity of the present fashion in evening dress seems to demand something important in the way of a coiffure decoration. A change of head-dress, moreover, has a great effect in making the same gown look different for various functions. It is a great advantage, therefore, for the girl with clever fingers to manufacture some dainty trifles of this kind. The illustrations afford some suggestions for pretty designs which can be easily carried out.

Illustration No. 1 shows a decoration consisting of a simple twist of pale blue satin ribbon passed on either side of the front through a jewelled ring. The rings should be cut out in buckram and wired at each edge, and be $3\frac{1}{4}$ inches in diameter when finished. They should be covered with the blue satin ribbon, and have a few jewels and beads sewn over them and around the edges. To keep them in position they are stitched on the ribbon.

Fig. I. A simple but charming decoration, consisting of a twist of satin ribbon passed on either side of the head through a jewelled ring

The second illustration depicts a very novel idea. A twist of silver gauze is passed around the hair and finished at one side of the back, under a knot of gauze with a hanging cluster of gold and silver fuchsias. To make the fuchsias, get some narrow gold cord and ravel a little piece about a couple of inches long, and double it in half to form the stamens. Join these to another piece of gold cord several inches long for the stalk. Take a little piece of gold cloth, thin but not transparent, fold it and gather it, and roll it around the stamens so that they show well below it. Just above tie a knot in the gold cord, and, above this again, stitch on four little petals of fine transparent silver gauze, folded on the cross so that they can be pulled out into the correct long shape. The knot in the cord is to make these petals stand out properly. Where the petals are gathered, they should be caught together in two places, one just

Fig. 2. A novel and pretty effect, gained by passing a twist of silver gauze round the hair and finishing it at one side with a cluster of gold and silver fuchsias

Fig. 3. A simple and classic style, in which a band of gold metallic moiré ribbon is arranged in a flat bow at the side, with a jewelled cabochon in the centre

57

above the other, to form the fat part of the calyx.

The third head-dress shown is simple, but very becoming to some wearers. It is composed of a band of gold metallic moiré ribbon arranged in a flat bow at one side. In the centre of this is a large gold, jewelled cabochon. To make this is an interesting task. First there is the buckram mould on which it is mounted to be evolved. Get the top of a wooden darner, wet a piece of buckram with boiling water, and fix it over this with the gummy side on the outside. Smooth,

it down evenly, and tie a piece of string around the base to help keep if in position while it is set in front of the fire on a plate to dry. When it is quite dry, fold the edges under inside over a fine wire, and sew this in place. The mould is now ready to cover with a piece of gold tissue. After that it can be decorated with any odd scraps of metallic trimming and beads to suit the taste of the worker, but it looks well to keep it all to different shades of gold, with just a touch of cut steel in the shape of the flat beads that can be bought by the string.

To be continued.

PRACTICAL LESSONS IN TAILORING
FOR HOME WORKERS AND OTHERS
By M. PRINCE BROWNE

Examiner in Dressmaking, Tailoring, French Pattern Modelling, Millinery, and Plain Needlework of the Teachers in Training at the University College of South Wales and Monmouthshire, Cardiff, the London Technical Examination Centre, etc. Author of " Up-to-date Dresscutting and Drafting," also " The Practical Work of Dressmaking and Tailoring."

Continued from page 642, Part 5

SIXTH LESSON. CUTTING OUT AND MAKING A COAT

Roll Collar (concluded)—How to Cut Out and Make a Coat—Placing the Pieces on the Material

THE edges of the collar having been turned down and tacked, and all superfluous material cut away from the corners that they may set as flat as possible, the raw edges must now be herringboned down to the canvas —the stitches must not be taken through to the material. It is not necessary to work this very neatly or to use silk. The collar must next be pressed. To do this, place it on a bare ironing or sleeve board, with the canvas uppermost, dip the tips of the fingers into water, damp it all over equally, and press it out flat with a tailor's goose.

Continue pressing the collar, and while doing so stretch the outer edge of the " fall " of the collar in the *length as much as possible* from one end to the other. Holding the iron with the right hand, stretch as hard as possible with the left ; then, holding the iron with the left hand, stretch as hard as possible with the right, that both ends may be stretched equally and exactly alike. Continue doing this until all the moisture has dried up from the board and the canvas has regained its stiffness.

Pressing the Collar

Take the collar off the board, and crease down sharply all along the curved line of running stitches—dividing the " stand " from the " fall "—with the finger and thumb ; hold the ends of the collar together, one over the other, forming the collar into a circle, with the " fall " outside. Dip the finger into water, and damp along the crease just made. Place the collar on the board with the " fall " downwards, and the " stand " to the right turning inwards. Hold the two ends together, one between the

thumb and forefinger, the other between the second and third finger of the left hand, and press the crease sharply down all round with the narrow end of the iron. Hold the collar in a circle all the time, lifting the iron constantly, and moving the collar round under it. Great care must be taken not to flatten the collar again, the crease *alone* requires to be pressed. The collar is now ready to be fixed on to a coat.

The worker having learned to make a " flap " pocket, and to pad and make a " roll " collar, can now apply the knowledge she has gained to the making of a coat like the one in the finished sketch.

How to Cut and Make a Coat

This useful little coat, designed to be worn with the skirt illustrated in the same sketch (instructions for the making of which are being given in the Lesson on Dressmaking), can be drafted direct on to the material from a good and well-fitting bodice pattern, and then cut out by the worker. No coat pattern is necessary.

Explanations of the Lines and Marks used in Drafting the Coat from the Bodice Pattern :

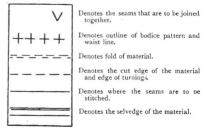

Denotes the seams that are to be joined together.

Denotes outline of bodice pattern and waist line.

Denotes fold of material.

Denotes the cut edge of the material and edge of turnings.

Denotes where the seams are to be stitched.

Denotes the selvedge of the material.

For adaptation to a coat it is better to have the bodice pattern modelled to a length of 7 inches below the waist, so that the size of the hips may be obtained.

How to Place the Pattern on the Material

Two and three-quarter yards of serge, 54 inches wide, will be required to make the coat as shown in the sketch. It should be of a firm make, not loose and " stretchy," or the seams will be crooked. The basque of the coat, measured from the waistline to the bottom, is 14 inches in depth. Place the piece of material on the table, folded lengthwise, the two selvedges together, and place the front of the bodice pattern on it at one end, with the front edge about 3 inches from the selvedge to allow for the revers, and extra width for the front of the *coat* (see diagram 1). Pin it smoothly to the material with ordinary pins, or through the material to the deal table or board with " push pins." (These pins are illustrated on page 72 in Part 1.) Take a piece of tailor's chalk, hold it upright, and outline the pattern close to the edge all round, and mark the waistline on each side. Take a tape measure, and hold the end of it between the thumb and forefinger of the right hand *on* the waistline of the front of the bodice pattern.

Take a piece of tailor's chalk in the left hand, and hold it upright in the tape measure exactly on the number denoting the length (14 inches) the basque is to be when finished. Mark round with the chalk held upright, working the hands slowly and simultaneously to the width required for the front, being careful to keep the tape tightly extended between the two hands. This gives the line for the bottom of the front of the coat.

From each side of the bodice pattern, draw with the square a straight line to the one just made.

To allow for the revers, draw lines on the material from the front to the selvedge, as shown on the diagram. The selvedge itself can be left on for the turning down the front edge.

This completes the outline for the front piece of the coat. Draw a second line about 1 inch beyond the outline of the side-seam for the turning.

For the shoulder, draw a second line about 1½ inches beyond the outline, as this is a " fitting seam."

Draw a second line, about 1½ inches from the bottom, for the turning up. Place the pattern of the side of the front in the position shown on the diagram. Outline the pattern close to the edge all round, and mark the waistline on each side. Measure the length for the basque (14 inches), and with the tape measure and piece of chalk draw the line for the bottom of the side in the same way as for the front.

From the *front* side of the bodice pattern draw with the square a straight line to the one just made, and from the *back* side draw a sloping line. To do this, place the square from the waist along the edge of the bodice pattern, and draw a line to the bottom of the

coat. This completes the outline of the side of the front.

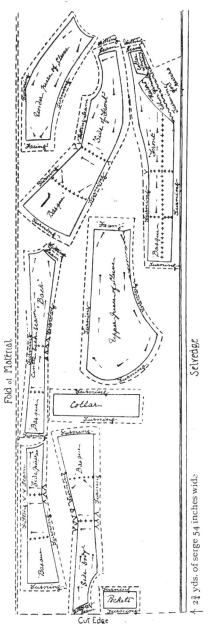

Diagram 1. Showing how the separate parts of the pattern for coat must be placed on material. When cutting out, the selvedge should be in front of the worker

59

Finished sketch of the coat, showing collar, revers, pocket. etc., as described. The making of the skirt is fully described and illustrated in the dressmaking lessons

Measure and mark for the turnings in the same way as the front.

Place the patterns of the " back," " side body," and " side-piece " on the material as shown in the diagram, and outline each piece all round near the edge.

A Coat is Made Longer Waisted than a Bodice

N.B.—A coat must always be longer waisted than a bodice, especially in the back and " side body," from 1 inch to 1½ inches, according to the figure. For a slight figure 1½ inches would not be too much ; for a stout figure 1 inch would be sufficient.

Add to the length for the basque 1 or 1½ inches (to lengthen the waist), and with the tape measure and piece of chalk draw the line for the bottom of each piece.

Draw a *straight* line for the front, and a *sloping* line for the back of each piece, in the same way as for the side of the front.

N.B.—As there is no " face " to a serge, the pieces can be placed up and down on it (see diagram). There is no fear of the pieces not matching, as they are being cut from the material folded double ; but as serge is a diagonal material, the bottom of the sleeve pattern must always be placed *straight* across the cut edge, as shown in the diagram. If this is not done it will be found that the " diagonal " will run across the one sleeve and down the other.

Outline the pattern of the sleeve, and draw a second line about an inch beyond it on the inner seam and round the top, and about 1½ inches for turning on the back seam (as this is the fitting seam), and draw a second line about 2 inches from the outline at the bottom for turning up.

N.B.—Tailors always leave this extra turning or " inlay " at the bottom of the sleeve to turn up, instead of " facing " a sleeve as dressmakers do.

The blank space left on the diagram represents the material left over for the " facing " of the " revers " and front (which should be cut in one piece), also for the straps round the sleeves. (See finished sketch.)

The " facing " for the front of the coat must be cut longer than from the bottom of the coat to the top of the " revers," because then the " revers " is turned back ; the " facing " of it should also form part of the " facing " of the collar, as shown by the dotted line in diagram. (This will appear in the next Lesson in Tailoring.)

N.B.—It is better to leave the cutting out of these " facings " until the coat is in a more advanced stage,—*i.e.*, until the fronts have been interlined with French canvas, the revers padded, and the edges of both turned in, the shoulder seams joined up, and the collar padded and put on. When all this has been done, the correct size and shape of the " facing " is more easily ascertained, and a diagram for cutting it out will be given in a future lesson.

Cut out all the pieces of the coat, sleeves, etc., carefully, on the *outer* lines (which denote the turnings). Unpin all the pieces of the bodice pattern ; do not *separate* the pieces of the material, but put a pin or two through each double piece, to keep them exactly together. Take a square and draw the waist line across each double piece of the coat from the chalk line on each side of the waist.

The double pieces for the collar and for the pocket-flaps can be put aside, as they are not required at present.

" Tailor-tack " through the double pieces on all the chalk lines denoting the outline of coat, waist line and sleeves, in order to reproduce these lines on the under pieces of the material. Instructions for " tailor-tacking " are given in the lesson on dressmaking.

To be continued.

PRACTICAL LESSONS IN DRESSMAKING

Continued from page 637, Part 5

By M. PRINCE BROWNE

Examiner in Dressmaking, Tailoring, French Pattern Modelling, Plain Needlework, and Millinery, of the Teachers in Training at the University College of South Wales and Monmouthshire, Cardiff; the London Higher Technical Examination Centres, etc.; First Class Diploma for Tailoring; Diploma of Honour for Dressmaking; Diploma of Merit of the Highest Order for Teaching; Silver Medallist, London Exhibition, 1900; Silver Medal, Franco-British Exhibition, 1908; Author of " Up-to-Date Dresscutting and Drafting," also " The Practical Work of Dressmaking and Tailoring."

SIXTH LESSON. A SIMPLE SKIRT—continued

THE " darts " must be about 5 inches long, and must be most carefully made.

Fit one side of the skirt only; the other side must be made to match when the skirt has been removed from the figure or dress-stand.

After the skirt has been fitted correctly on the one side, take a piece of tailor's chalk and make marks on *each* side of the two darts and a mark across the bottom of each; remove the pins, and place the skirt flat on the table, right side uppermost. Hold the chalk upright between the thumb and first finger, and perfect the outline of the dart, keeping it to the size denoted by the chalk-marks and to the length shown by the mark across the bottom of the dart. It must be sloped as gradually as possible towards the point, or there will be fulness at the bottom. The most accurate way of marking the darts on to the second side is by " tailor tacking," and, although this is not the method usually adopted by dressmakers, it is by far the most correct and satisfactory way, and if carefully carried out ensures the two sides being exactly alike.

Fold the skirt in half—right side out—and place it flat on the table with the side on which the darts are marked uppermost, pin it together along the top, and stick one pin, *downwards*, in the centre of each dart.

Thread a needle with a *long* length of white tacking cotton—or cotton of a contrasting colour to the material—double the cotton, but do not make a knot at the end of it. Stick the needle in at the *lowest* point of one of the darts (see Diagram 1) and make a small, running stitch through the *two* sides of the skirt *exactly on* the chalk line—leave an end about half an inch long instead of a knot—and make another small running stitch on the chalk line—about half an inch from the first—leaving a *loose loop* between. Continue these stitches to the top of the dart, and cut off the thread about half an inch beyond the last one. Make another row of these running stitches *on* the chalk line down the other side of the dart, leaving an end of about half an inch—when making the first stitch—instead of a knot, as shown by the diagram.

Tailor tack the second dart in the same way. Unpin the skirt, draw the two sides of it slightly apart, and cut the double tacking threads—which hold them together—with a short, sharp pair of scissors without drawing any of the threads out of the material.

N.B.—Blunt scissors are apt to catch the threads and pull them out, and with long scissors there is danger of snipping the material.

When all the threads have been cut, the darts should appear traced by a line of short double threads on both sides of the skirt exactly to correspond, as shown in Diagram 2.

N.B.—The seams, corrections, etc., of the two sides of any garment can be made exactly alike by being tailor tacked.

Take the skirt off the table, turn it to the wrong side, and form *each* of the darts by bringing the two lines of tailor tacking *exactly* together *from the top to the point*. Pin *each* dart together, being careful that the pins are *on* the line of tacking on *both* sides.

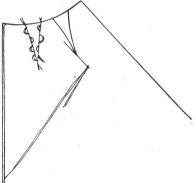

Diagram 1. Tailor tacking the darts. This is the best method of ensuring the accuracy of the darts

Thread a needle with single tacking cotton —white or coloured—make a knot at the end, and tack *each* dart from the top to the point exactly on the line of tailor tacking. This tacking should be done rather neatly, and *most carefully* and *gradually* finished off, so that no fulness may be left at the point of the dart.

Before stitching the darts, remove all the short threads of the tailor tacking, as it is very difficult to do so after the machine-stitching has been done. The darts must *all* be stitched from the top downwards, in order to work the point gradually off to nothing. If worked from the point upwards the first stitch would *have* to be made on the material, and a little pleat would thereby be formed in the skirt under each dart. The two seams which are already tacked must now be machine-stitched from the top downwards, and, after the tacking-threads have been taken out, place the skirt—wrong side uppermost—on a skirtboard, dip the tips of the fingers in water, and damp one of the seams before pressing.

N.B.—The turnings in this style of seam— shown in the skirt of the finished sketch in the Tailoring Lesson, page 758—must *not* be separated and pressed open, but should be turned the same way—towards the front of the skirt.

How to Damp and Press the Seams

Press the seam *well* from the top downwards. The iron should not be constantly lifted and put down again, but moved very gradually all along the seam, and it must not be hot enough to scorch, as it should be allowed to remain some time on the seam ; it is the weight and time given to pressing that ensure good results.

The damping must not be commenced

right through the double turnings that are on the wrong side.

Machine-stitch—with silk—down each side of the front, about three-eighths of an inch from the seam ; these seams should now have the appearance of being lapped.

Joining the Back of Skirt

The back of the skirt must now be joined up. To do this fold the skirt in half—wrong side out—and place it flat on the table with the two edges exactly meeting ; pin them together from the top downwards, allowing the weight of the skirt to rest on the table to prevent stretching the back seam, one side of which is more apt to stretch than the other. Both sides must be kept exactly the same length—they were cut exactly the same size—and the turnings must, therefore, be *made* to meet, both at the top and at the bottom. The hang of the skirt will be spoiled if one side is stretched and then cut off to make it the same length as the other.

Measure one inch and a half from the edge and make a mark, continue to measure

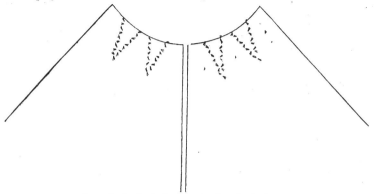

Diagram 2. Showing the darts when the tailor-tacking has been cut

until the iron is ready heated, and one seam only must be damped at a time, or the other seams will shrink while the first is being pressed.

Damp and press the second seam in the same way, then cut the turnings of the darts down the centre and as near to the point as possible.

Separate the turning of one of the darts and damp and press the seam of it *open* and *quite flat.*

N.B.—Special care must be taken to thoroughly damp the extreme point, and the iron must be allowed to remain on it until all the moisture has dried up from the board on which it is being pressed, so that *if* there is any fulness at the point it may be shrunk away.

Damp and press the three other darts in the same way.

Turn the skirt over, and place it on the board again—right side uppermost—and tack down each side of the front about a quarter of an inch from the seam, taking the needle

and mark at intervals all down the back of the skirt, and with two tailor's squares placed together draw one long line for the back seam—passing through these marks— to ensure its being tacked and stitched perfectly straight. Cut a strip of linen, selvedgewise, about half an inch wide and the length of the skirt—a piece of tape will do equally well. Place it *over* and all *along* the chalk line, and tack it through the double material all down the back of the skirt.

Machine stitch down the seam from the top of the skirt to the bottom.

N.B.—The strip of linen or tape stitched in with the seam will prevent it stretching.

Take out the tacking, damp the seam, and press it open, following the instructions given for pressing.

The back seam of a skirt should always be pressed open, even when the other seams are " lapped "—the skirt would appear crooked if the back seam were " lapped."

To be continued.

Printed in Great Britain
by Amazon

38294332R00040